Climate Crisis and Consciousness

Climate crisis disrupts the beliefs, values and behaviours of contemporary societies, sparking potential for radical changes in culture and consciousness. Drawing upon her experience as a Jungian psychotherapist and a researcher in the field of climate psychology, Sally Gillespie writes about the challenges, dilemmas, opportunities and transformations of engaging with climate and ecological crises.

Many factors shape how we understand and respond to the existential threats of climate crisis. This accessible book with its discussions about worldviews, cultural myths, emotional resilience, social connectedness, nature relatedness and collective action explores consciousness change in those most engaged with climate issues. Calling upon the words and stories of many people, including Indigenous leaders, ecologists, campaigners, writers and philosophers, Gillespie encourages us to enter into climate conversations to forge emotional resilience, ecological consciousness and inspired action.

With its unique focus on the psychological experience of facing into the climate crisis, this warm and supportive book offers companionship and sustenance for anyone who wants to be alive to our natural world and to the existential challenges of today. It is an essential resource for counsellors, psychotherapists, social workers and other helping professionals, as well as climate campaigners, policy makers, educators, scientists and researchers.

Sally Gillespie, PhD, worked as a Jungian psychotherapist for over twenty years before undertaking doctoral research in climate psychology at Western Sydney University. She now lectures, and facilitates workshops, on climate psychology and ecopsychology. A former president of the Jung Society of Sydney, Sally is a member of Psychology for a Safe Climate, the Climate Psychology Alliance and the Climate Wellbeing Network.

Climate Crisis and Consciousness

Re-imagining Our World and Ourselves

Sally Gillespie

Routledge
Taylor & Francis Group

LONDON AND NEW YORK

First published 2020
by Routledge
2 Park Square, Milton Park, Abingdon, Oxon OX14 4RN

and by Routledge
52 Vanderbilt Avenue, New York, NY 10017

Routledge is an imprint of the Taylor & Francis Group, an informa business

British Library Cataloguing-in-Publication Data
A catalogue record for this book is available from the British Library

Library of Congress Cataloging-in-Publication Data
A catalog record has been requested for this book

ISBN: 978-0-367-36532-5 (hbk)
ISBN: 978-0-367-36534-9 (pbk)
ISBN: 978-0-429-34681-1 (ebk)

Typeset in Times New Roman
by Swales & Willis, Exeter, Devon, UK

for the young ones
everywhere
and
for Jonathan
always

Contents

Acknowledgements

The roots of this book stretch back to my PhD research at Western Sydney University. It was a rich experience, informed and supported by many. My supervisors Dr Brenda Dobia, Dr David Wright and Dr Catherine Camden-Pratt, were skilled mentors whose contributions, encouragement and belief in my work sustained me through my research and beyond. An enormous thank you to them, and to Linda Cairnes, Stella Hristias, Jonathan Marshall, Liz Morgan, Vince Polidano, Erla Ronan, Lisa Roberts, Kim Schavey, Mark Singer and Christian Zuur for all the ways they brought their insights and enthusiasm to my research and writing.

I am very fortunate to belong to three climate psychology networks, all of which sustain and inform my work and wellbeing. Many people quoted in this book belong to the Climate Psychology Alliance. Their website and mailing list is a rich source of knowledge, inquiry and in-depth discussions about the growing field of climate psychology for which I am most grateful. A special thank you to CPA members Paul Hoggett and Rosemary Randall for their ongoing interest, encouragement and inspiration. Big thanks also to Psychology for a Safe Climate in Melbourne, for their stimulating conferences, workshops and writings, and to PSC convenor Carol Ride for her generous support and friendship. And hearty thanks to Merle Conyer, Rosey Faire, Beth Hill, Nic Thornton and Christie Wilson from the Climate Wellbeing Network for companionship, care and conversations.

A major theme of this book is the importance of supportive and exploratory conversations to develop and maintain a healthy engagement with climate issues. I am enormously grateful for the many conversations that have sustained and stimulated me through the process of writing this book. I would especially like to thank my very dear friends in the Earth Climate Dreams group: Susannah Benson, Bonnie Bright, Veronica Goodchild, Jeff Kiehl, Jonathan Marshall and Robert Romanyshyn. Our years of conversations and dream sharing have been a lifeline, a joy, and so much more. And a warm thank you to Ken McLeod and everyone in the Anthropocene Transition Network Dialogue Circle, for many spacious hours of reflective dialogue exploring the times and world we live in.

A deep bow of acknowledgement to Indigenous cultures worldwide for their profound and well-tested teachings, resilience and leadership in ecological understanding and care. To my great good fortune, I grew up in Aotearoa New Zealand, learning something of Māori culture which continues to hearten and inspire me. These days I live on Gadigal-Wangal country in Sydney, Australia where the Aboriginal traditional owners hold an extraordinary knowledge of country developed over more than 60,000 years. I am deeply grateful to them for all that I have learnt and am yet to learn from their culture and their elders, past, present and emerging.

A big thank you to Judith Pickering for her generous initiative in introducing me to Routledge. My thanks to all the Routledge team, particularly Lucinda Knight and Vijila Stephens for their warm support and Heather Evans for being such a skilled and delightful editorial assistant. While writing this book I attended monthly meetings of the Non Fiction Writers Group of the New South Wales Writer's Centre, convened by Suzanne Little. Enormous thanks to Suzanne and all the participants in the group who gave me such skilled and helpful feedback on my writing style, along with their enthusiasm for this book.

My husband Jonathan Marshall, always my most tireless and passionate supporter, read and edited the entire manuscript, more than once. This book is so much the better for his academic expertise, wise words and loving nature. As is my life. My gratitude, appreciation and love for him goes far beyond words.

Heartiest thanks to all my family and friends who have cheered me on. To Brigid Lowry, the hugest thank you for reading each chapter as I wrote it. Your feedback, sound writerly advice, and many supportive messages have kept me going in so many ways. A special thank you to Suzanne Bartos, Denise Corrigan, Maria Hole, Maggie Hyde and David Watson for their thoughtful comments on the chapters they read. And to Lindel Barker-Revell, Annie Bell, Alicia, Quique and Gerry Fox, Wayne Gillespie, Stephanie Dowrick, Deborah Bonham, Brenda Dobia, Liz Morgan, Lea Dalgleish, Sue

Callanan, Annie Foy and Ella Dreyfus, a loving thank you for being there and caring about this book's progress.

My parents, Heather and Mick Gillespie, both passed away while I was writing this book. Their spirit remains with me, as does their love for our world, which they gifted to me along with their unfailing love and support. This book and so much of what I care about is nourished by my memories of them, for which I am forever grateful.

Introduction
Sea change

Yesterday, on my way home from the osteopath, I drove past ten-million-dollar waterfront mansions teetering on the edge of the sea. Giant waves and king tides had obliterated their gardens and undermined their foundations during the previous weekend's "horror storm." Now these seaside palaces were empty, taped off by emergency services. Police dotted the kerbside, chatting in the sun, watching engineers and insurance assessors come and go, while locals craned their necks on the way to the shops.

Like many, I used to fantasise how climate change would play out. The dangers, although deeply alarming, seemed far off. But now they are here, creeping up to our doorsteps. Floods, bushfires, droughts and bleached corals all feature in this week's papers, and each report makes mention of the increased risks of climate change. Not so many years ago, references to climate change in the aftermath of natural disasters were quickly branded as political opportunism. These days they are fairly common, although rarely prominent.

Today *The Sydney Morning Herald*'s editorial commented that in view of climate change and ongoing beach erosion "managed retreats [from the ocean] remain a sensible alternative" to clinging on to beachside homes.[1] On another page, there is a report that wind energy generation records had been smashed due to the blustery weather, temporarily halting the climb of carbon emissions.[2] The surreal is becoming mundane, as we topple over the edge of our known world into a sea change of global proportions.

I cannot recall the exact moment when I became conscious of global warming, but I vividly remember reading George Monbiot's book *Heat* in 2006, and thinking that I would never look at the world or my life again in the same way. I accepted the evidence that our planet was hotting up and that every human alive, including me, was in some way implicated in its causes, effects and its solutions. Ever since, a good proportion of my life has been spent coming to terms with this and figuring out how to live well in this overheating world of ours.

Working as a psychotherapist I became intrigued by what happens at an emotional level when climate disruption crosses our radar. In 2009, I began writing a journal about my own and others' responses to global warming. I could see a lot of defence mechanisms at play. Not only in other people's passionate denials and attacks on those "scaremongering Greenies" and "dishonest scientists," but also in my own attempts to convince myself that climate change might not be that bad, or that there was little I could do about it. Writing helped me to recognise and navigate my way through my denials and disavowals about the climate crisis. It also helped me to find my sea legs for the emotional ups and downs of being in a disrupted world where climate stability and biodiversity are becoming extinct.

My journal also recorded my own life changes. I had been practising as a Jungian psychotherapist for over twenty years, but my energy and health were waning. My focus shifted from the therapy room into the life of the world. After a dream of earth shaking proportions, which you will hear about in Chapter 1, I knew that I had to change my life. In 2010 I started a PhD investigating the psychological terrain of my own and others' engagement with climate change. Not long after, I closed my private practice. My personal climate had well and truly changed.

In my new world, I recruited volunteers to join me in a discussion group about our psychological responses to climate issues. This group comprised a mix of activists, artists, policymakers and community workers, all willing to delve into their personal responses to global heating and related ecological disasters. We met throughout 2011. Our discussions propelled us into fertile territory, as we explored what our thoughts, feeling and actions were in response to climate disruption. What we found was that our responses were generally as complex, varied and charged as the phenomenon of climate change itself.[3]

In order to capture something of the flavour and focus of our conversations, I drew up a map of the major themes that emerged over our twelve meetings. I named imaginary continents after our hottest topics, including "Relating to Earth," "Values" and "Survival." Each continent had imaginary geographical features, named after phrases lifted directly from our conversations, such as "Bamboozled Bay," "Not Noticing Coast" and "Nitty Gritty Rocks." It was a relief to give form and containment to so many thoughts and feelings that had been bubbling away beneath the surface. The map acknowledged the challenges of living in our climate disrupted world while recognising the discoveries and adventures emerging within this experience.

When our research group started meeting, there was a collective sigh of relief around the room. Person after person talked about their feelings of isolation, and their struggles to find receptive people and places to discuss the psychological dimensions of being aware of climate issues. Even the activists and those directly working in the climate change field, spoke of how circumscribed their conversations often were when it came to discussing their emotional responses. Thankfully, this is now changing. Eco-anxiety, eco-grief and eco-despair are commonly acknowledged and written about in the more progressive media outlets. However, the problem for many of us remains that initiating and sustaining conversations about climate crisis is difficult. Sex is an easier dinner table topic than melting glaciers. Too often the conversation halts with uneasy jokes about rising sea levels and a quick change of subject. People are left stranded, often not knowing what to think, because of the lack of opportunity to talk freely about the confusions, fears, frustrations and griefs that are a part of the climate crisis territory. When non-engagement becomes the norm, it not only stymies action, but also stifles a liveliness that springs from consciously engaging with the world as it is, and ourselves as we are.

At the end of the research, many participants spontaneously remarked that they felt they had "grown up" through our conversations. It seemed that facing into climate disruption and related issues had brought us to a better place in ourselves and the world, despite the fact we had become more aware of the challenges. Our discussions threw up fresh understandings which helped ease our confusions and dreads. We became less flummoxed by our fluctuating emotions, as we learnt how to take better care of ourselves and how to keep our engagement lively.

Since then, I have continued to listen and talk to anyone willing to discuss climate concerns and what they mean for them. While there are no fixed patterns, I do recognise common experiences, concerns and responses which are often overlooked in climate conversations. My aim in writing this book is to share discussions and stories about the psychological and emotional dimensions of climate engagement. In particular, I want to talk about how consciousness changes when we do engage with the full knowledge and implications of climate crisis and the many other human-driven ecological destructions that accompany this phenomenon. As Albert Einstein famously said, we cannot solve a problem by addressing it from the same level of thinking that caused it. To even begin to deal with climate crisis, responsibly and effectively, we need to engage in the work of changing consciousness. This is particularly true for those of us who have been educated within Western belief systems with all their assumptions about how humans are separate and superior to the natural world.

While most climate discussions tend to focus on action and/or inaction, the stories which most interest me also tune into feelings, values, beliefs, identities and worldviews. In this book I draw upon many people's accounts of their tussles with existential questions about death, transience, uncertainty, vulnerability, connectedness and the nature of the world provoked by climate emergency and ecological collapse. These are juicy questions. I have come to believe that engaging with them is one of the most potent and compelling catalysts for psychological growth today.

One of my favourite writers, Rebecca Solnit, has observed that there are two disparate meanings of "lost": one involves "the familiar falling away" while the other "is about the unfamiliar appearing in which case ... the world has become larger than your knowledge of it."[4] Many climate discussions focus on the first meaning of lost, the one in which we risk being stripped of everything we have come to take for granted, from reliable rainfall to aeroplane travel. However, I believe it is the second meaning of lost that more fundamentally addresses the challenge of living on a rapidly heating planet. This definition highlights the awareness that we can never fully know or control our infinitely complex and unpredictable world. This is the feeling of lost we must learn to consciously live within.

Relinquishing human fantasies of omnipotence stimulates fresh observations and experimentations. When we leave an illusory view of the world behind, we open up a life of discovery. To get to this enlivened place, we must travel through a transitional zone between an old worldview and a new one. Psychotherapist Ginette Paris observes that the terrain between an old myth, or worldview, and a new one often feels like a "deadly zone, where feelings of loss loom large and confusions abound."[5] She suggests that depth psychology provides an illuminating map for such a transition because of its ability to recognise the dynamic phases of transformation that occur when consciousness changes. Depth psychology encourages us to leave behind habitual and restrictive views of ourselves and lives. It urges us to get lost by heading towards the unknown and heeding what lies in the margins of life and of consciousness, including dreams, fantasies and visions. There is no fixed "right place" within depth psychology's map of consciousness change, but there are pathways that can take us through challenging truths and that can yield expansive views. This book contains many personal reflections from a wide range of people on the experience of engaging with climate upheaval and related issues. Different people face into different aspects of the journey in different ways and at different times. There is no one right way to negotiate the times we are in, or the changes of consciousness that press upon us. What matters is the willingness to be open to the unfamiliar and uncertain, developing awareness, relatedness and compassion along the way.

The changes we need to make to live well on planet Earth are as much psychological as physical. This book is one of many individual and collective responses to the psychological challenges and opportunities of engaging with climate crisis. Sharing stories, thoughts, feelings and dreams (both day and night) in response to ecological destructions is a crucial part of illuminating this process. Without the experience and company of others it is easy to feel swamped when facing into the stormy waves of our world's growing climate emergency. With others, we can create sturdy vessels for transformation that can navigate emerging worlds, beliefs and identities attuned to ecological life and death.

In the pages ahead you will find discussions and stories about a wide range of dilemmas and opportunities that open up when we recognise our world is in a deepening state of climate emergency. Chapter 1 approaches the psychological dimensions of climate engagement through a discussion about worldviews, myths and consciousness change. Chapter 2 introduces some of the major issues of climate engagement and climate psychology while Chapters 3 and 4 reflect on human embeddedness within the natural world and the development of ecological consciousness. Chapter 5 explores how this consciousness can be enacted within daily life while Chapter 6 focuses on the psychological dimensions of climate action and campaigns. In the final chapter, I look at the creative role of myths, stories, dreams and art in evolving worldviews, ethics and social change movements which are responsive to climate crisis and growing eco-logical consciousness. You can read this book in chronological order, or dive into single chapters as they interest you. If you do read the book straight through, you will find that major themes are explored from many perspectives within differing contexts.

While I make reference to the science, politics, economics and technologies associated with climate change, this is not my focus as it is well covered elsewhere. My focus is on introducing you to the psychological responses and transformations that engaging with climate issues can spark as it disrupts how we think about our-selves, our lives and our world. At the end of the book, I suggest literature and resources that can take you further into both research on climate psychology and the development of ecological consciousness.

It is human nature to mistrust and avoid change and disruption, just as it is the nature of life to deliver them. Through my experience with depth psychology, I have learnt to recognise within disruptive times and crises points powerful opportunities for breaking out of constricting habitual behaviours and views. We have collectively reached a time of extreme disruption in human history and Earth's history. The losses are severe and worsening. We can resist facing these catastrophes and become ever more caught up in unsustainable and destructive fantasies which drive species extinctions including very possibly our own, or we can individually and collectively face into the crisis. While there are no guaranteed outcomes, the latter choice lays the foundations for meaningful lives meaning, care and connection.

In their reflections on the question of how should we live in this time, Dahr Jamail and Barbara Cecil write of the potency of refusing "to walk in the mainstream western herd, conforming to expectations and values that have ultimately ravaged the Earth," and of entering into healing collaborations "strangely rich with a new brand of fulfilment and unprecedented intimacy with the Earth and one another."[6] In this book you will find many reflec-tions and stories about the ways people are living and transforming within the realms of climate emergency and ecological collapse. As you read on, may you find inspiration for your own cultivation of ecological consciousness and commitment to restorative actions in the good company of our Earth and her wondrous ways of being.

Notes

1 Editorial. (2016, Jun 9). *The Sydney Morning Herald*, p. 12.
2 Hannam, P. (2016, Jun 9). Blowy days push wind power supply to record level. *The Sydney Morning Herald*, p. 4.
3 For a more detailed description of this research see Gillespie, S. (2019). Researching climate engagement: Collaborative conversations and consciousness change. In P. Hoggett (Ed.), *Climate psychology: From indifference to disaster*. Basingstoke, UK: Palgrave Macmillan, pp. 107–127.
4 Solnit, R. (2005). *A field guide to getting lost*. London, UK: Canongate, p. 22.
5 Paris, G. (2008). *Wisdom of the psyche: Depth psychology after neuroscience*. Hove, UK: Routledge, p. 83.
6 Jamail, D. & Cecil, B. (2019, Mar 4). Rethink activism in the face of catastrophic biological collapse. Retrieved from *Truthout*. https://truthout.org /articles/climate-collapse-is-on-the-horizon-we-must-act-anyway/.

Chapter 1

Departing familiar shores

Dropping to Earth

How we see our world and how it is, are not the same thing. When the anthropologist Gregory Bateson said that "the major problems in the world are the result of the difference between how nature works and the way people think,"[1] he was not referring to the climate crisis, although he might well have been. For the problems of global warming have crept up on many who never thought that burning fossil fuels or clearing forests could change our planetary atmosphere. Only now, as temperature records tumble and climate disasters intensify, are perceptions of our world changing, as we collectively stumble into consciousness about Earth's climate and our place within it.

Changing consciousness, whether personal or collective, disrupts our sense of reality. Information about climate crisis can induce a weird feeling of unreality as we try to reconcile our familiar, daily life with the increasing risks and costs of climate disruption. It is often hard to know what to think. But perhaps this is just what is needed: an interruption of habitual thinking, in order to absorb new understandings about how our planet works and how we live. Facing into the dangers, losses and griefs of climate crisis changes consciousness, discrediting modernist fantasies which leave us off-balance and off-planet. In their stead are a whole raft of new realities to grapple with, ranging from the geophysical to the psychological. How we live cannot stay the same. To ride the stormy waves of our heating planet, we must think, feel and act in radically new ways.

My sea change in response to climate disruption began in 2008, when I organised a panel about depth psychology and climate change for the Sydney Jung Society. It went well, but life was busy. It was time, I thought, to move on to the next thing. But then I had a dream which felt more like a vision. It was a terrifying depiction of global chaos caused by climate disruption. In my dream I swung on a rope above the Earth as land masses shifted around beneath me. I saw continents sinking beneath rising seas. Millions of people in the oceans desperately attempted to cling to fast disappearing land. Somehow I knew I had to join them. I let go of the rope and dropped into this catastrophe, becoming one of many attempting to hold on to the heaving shores. In the midst of this horror, a desperate poodle swam into my arms. I cared for my newfound companion as best I could, while feeling the futility of everyone's struggle to survive.

I awoke from my dream with a thumping heart, warm in bed on a cold winter's night. Urgent questions pressed in on me: "How do I respond to this? How can I respond to this?" I was dazed by the "shock and awe" experience of dropping into an apocalyptic world. Any possibility of distancing myself from climate change reports collapsed. My dream had catapulted me out of my old life and view of the world. I shook for the vulnerability of all beings on Earth, as my consciousness opened up to the realities of collective fate.

I did not believe my dream was precognitive or prophetic in a literal sense, but I did feel that my world, the one I knew as a reality, was ending. My dream crashed through denials and rationalisations, breaching the walls of habitual thought and rupturing foundational beliefs about my personal autonomy and independence. I felt in my gut that I had to acknowledge the full seriousness of global warming, and that, in one way or another, I would spend the rest of my life acting in response.

For most of my adult life I had recorded and worked with my dreams, guided by the teachings of Carl Jung, a pioneer of modern dream analysis. Jung wrote that dreams about the world or social concerns did not belong to the dreamer, but had a collective meaning and "a character which forces people instinctively to tell them."[2] This is how my dream felt, even though my psychotherapist mind could readily conjure up dream interpretations relevant to my personal life at the time. But to restrict my dream within such a narrow view felt dismissive of both my instincts and of the world out there. My dream demanded an acknowledgement of the ways personal and collective realities are intertwined. It captured the ways that my growing awareness of climate disruption had pitched my consciousness into an irrevocably disordered world where my old and familiar life and ways of thinking were impossible.

Over the next few years I had further dreams, which related to, and extended, the experience of my "big dream." All contained some reference to climate disruption and/or ecological collapse and were set in, or around, water. In each dream, I was approached by an animal who looked for care and connection. In one, I gazed into a stormy sea, eagerly anticipating the end of the human race and, with this, the restoration of the health of the oceans. But, then a thirsty, bedraggled and crusty-skinned seal unexpectedly leapt into my arms, jolting me into the present. My mind abandoned its bleak and guilty imaginings in order to work out how to best care for this desperate creature. I realised that human presence, not absence, was needed in response to ecological destructions.

This series of climate change dreams navigated me through a sea of feelings. Over time, waves of despair, guilt, judgement, grief and con-fusion made way for currents of tenderness, connection, delight, wonder and love. In 2012, nearly four years after my initial dream, I had two successive dreams which brought some sense of resolution. In the first, I swam in the ocean circled by two seals and a dolphin who all looked deeply into my eyes before the dolphin reached forward with its snout and touched my arm. In the second, I travelled to the United States and walked along a waterfront when a seal swam up close to greet me. I gazed back, marvelling at its rodent-like features, golden eyes and grey mottled skin. Other people arrived, joining me in this communion between human and animal. In both of these dreams I felt pulled into a full seeing, and being seen, by the animals who approached me. No longer panicked, guilty, or inattentive, I was able to move into relationship with the animal/other at home in its world, and into a consciousness focused on the present. I could share my growing animal relatedness in the final dream, when other people joined me in the "United States" (a most wonderful dream pun!). Taken together, my dreams felt like a kind of initiation. They brought me face to face with my human self, my animal relations and my place in the world. Both in dream and waking life, I found my way from hopelessness and horror to commitment and care.

Learning to be with human, and other-than-human, beings, in today's world is a lesson in humility, grounding and compassion. It requires accepting our own and others' flawed humanity and animal nature, along with the beauty, terror, vulnerability and resilience of life. It's a daily challenge which I often fail, but cannot forget, as I learn to swim in the currents of dilemmas stirred up by climate disruption, looking for connection with others while heading towards the shores of wise action.

Disintegrating worldviews

When our view of the world changes, we change. And so do the personal and cultural myths we tell about ourselves, others and our world. Myths are the underlying, and mostly unconscious guiding stories of our lives, which shape how we understand and live. Climate crisis and other ecological disruptions are breaking apart established worldviews, and their accompanying myths, catapulting us out of habitual ways of understanding the world. Familiar truisms no longer convince or reassure us, as former Australian Prime Minister Tony Abbott found out when his enthusiastic statement that "coal is good for humanity" was widely ridiculed. Coal mining, that heroic enterprise of the Industrial Age, is no longer seen as compatible with a viable future. Nor is growth necessarily good or increasing GDP a marker of a nation's wellbeing. Social narratives and visions are transforming as our awareness of the impact of human activities on global ecosystems grows.

The fact that there have been deep pockets of resistance to climate action bears testament to the fierceness with which we guard old myths, and the beliefs that they sustain. This is especially so when they feel integral to defining personal identity, status and feelings of belonging. Where most people see opportunity and regeneration in abandoning fossil fuels and developing renewable energies, the climate change denialist perceives multiple threats, loss of security and an undermining of visions of the future. When climate campaigner George Marshall met up with Texan Tea Party activists, he found that their major fear was that climate related policies will impose governmental control over their lives: as one Tea Party activist put it, "The passion is not that we cover our ears with our hands and don't want to hear the facts. The passion is we don't want to be controlled."[3] The mythic narrative trumps scientific data.

The highest levels of climate crisis denial flourish amongst older people, particularly those identified with right-wing libertarian free market ideologies.[4] This group of people hears all talk of climate change as a threat to cherished values, allegiances and lifestyles. The more scientific evidence of climate crisis is shown to this group, the more convinced they become of its falsehood. This escalating denial is a way of reducing "cognitive dissonance," where the unconscious need to safeguard precious worldviews outweighs reasoned thought and direct observation. This is why throwing scientific evidence at dogged denialists never works. But, George Marshall suggests, telling the story of climate crisis in different ways might just cut through, if we can understand the values that underpin the worldviews of any given audience. The more we understand the myths and beliefs of those we want to communicate with, the better the chance we can find some points of entry and connection, as later chapters explore further.

It takes time to evolve new worldviews and to develop the cultural stories, or myths, that sustain them. Myths are imaginative templates which unconsciously shape our perceptions of, and relationship to, our world. The great mythologist Joseph Campbell wrote eloquently about how we are born into myths and are formed by them. Some forty years ago, Campbell wrote that "the only mythology that is valid today is the mythology of the planet – and we don't have such a mythology."[5] He believed, however, that when future myths arose, they would speak about the importance of developing individual maturity within a global society through holding a conscious positive relationship to nature and cosmos. Ask almost any child today about our planet, and they will talk about the need for all of us to take care of our Earth by living in ways that do not pollute its atmosphere and oceans. As I finish writing this book, hundreds of thousands of school students around the world are taking to the streets demanding action on climate with placards reading "Save our planet, save our future," "We are all in the same boat, stop drilling holes in it," "Global warning," "We can't drink oil, we can't eat money."[6] Their signs tell us that a global myth of alarm and danger, and care and respect is being born.

While we can never live free of myths, we can transform the ones we live by through questioning the viability and validity of their underlying values and imaginings. Usually it takes a serious challenge or crisis to provoke such demanding work. At a personal level, the breakdown of marriage or major illness can dismantle beliefs about who we are and what life is, just as, at a collective level, acts of terrorism or an environmental disaster can tear apart old assumptions. When old givens crumble, we stumble into a confused and chaotic time of transition. As much as we would like to, we cannot deliberately adopt new and better myths. Such deep change has to develop over time, working its way through the unconscious. This very human journey of transformation is a perennial source of fascination for us, the key dynamic in so much of our literature, film and reality television shows.

In today's world, the media and the creative arts seethe with debates about the "truths" of capitalism, globalisation, social democracy, scientific method and many other cultural bastions, as old myths are questioned in the light of present challenges. This questioning may feel far from our personal lives, but when the underlying problems reveal themselves in a way that impacts us, our ground of beliefs shakes ominously. Kim Schavey, a former lawyer from the United States, told me that when she first encountered information about the seriousness of climate change at a professional conference she attended in 2007, it triggered "a very grief filled time [of] being with this new reality." She started studying chaos theory and evolutionary science, and came to the conclusion that it was "pretty much impossible to continue with my life as it was." Shedding her old priorities and goals, she left the United States, exchanged her professional career for activist work, and decided not to have children. As Kim's vision of the world transformed, so did her life and identity.

When climate crisis crashes into consciousness it is just the beginning of the story; that point of disruption which reveals former assumptions and myths as fantasies and lies. Once the horror of Bluebeard's bloody chamber has been revealed, there is no choice but to live with the awareness of past destructions, present dangers and the necessity for action, even though we have not developed a new way to live yet. This is a chaotic time of global crisis and transformation. New and shocking understandings are being broadcast, fertilising emerging myths that narrate existential crises. In his response to contemporary global crises, the philosopher Jonathan Lear muses, "Perhaps if we could give a name to our shared sense of vulnerability, we could find better ways to live with it."[7]

Climate science highlights our "shared sense of vulnerability" in entirely new ways. Ongoing revelations about the interdependence of all life forms on Earth regularly shake my world. When I read about how warming and acidifying seas are causing an explosion of jellyfish, mass bleaching of coral, and the closure of fisheries, I am confronted by a chain of cascading disruptions. One part of me would like to forget or dismiss this new-found knowledge as unfortunate, or unlikely to affect me or those I care about, but such denials diminish me and our world, and are increasingly untenable as climate destructions become more visible and widespread. Instead, like so many others, I feel compelled to expand my consciousness, groping my way towards an ecological worldview that names and gives meaning to connections and vulnerabilities within this emerging view of the global web of life. My own questioning of myself, my society and our world has catapulted me into a voyage of discovery which I am grateful for, despite the horror and grief I feel. Through engaging with climate issues, I have developed a passion for learning about the miraculous interconnected processes that shape our planet and ourselves. I am also finding new life in shedding habits of thinking and living that on examination have been more deadening than inspiring.

Maturing myths

Understanding the fatal consequences of climate disruption for species and individuals, human and otherwise, throws us into uncharted seas. For many, the first myths that emerge around climate crisis are narratives of despair which place apocalypse just around the corner. Research within many countries consistently shows that there is a rising rate of pessimism about the future of human civilisation, and indeed of humanity itself. There is plenty of evidence that shows we are already in a time of "climate emergency" and "climate chaos." Nevertheless there is a narrow window of opportunity for crucial choices to be made and effective actions to be taken. We already have the technologies and knowhow to transition from fossil fuelled societies and to protect and create carbon sinks. What we need to cultivate is the courage to challenge unconscious assumptions and beliefs that lock us into maintaining the status quo of fossil fuel use, land clearing, agricultural and dietary practices, economic expansion, consumerist lifestyles and many other bastions of modern industrial societies.

In order to do this we need to question the myths we presently live by, asking: Where do our stories about our world come from? How do they envision myself and all other life forms? What effects are they having on myself and others, intended and unintended? Can they sustain myself and future generations? Do they offer meanings, inspiration and guidance for responding wisely and lovingly to the unique challenges and opportunities of our times?

The more consciously we reflect on what limits, motivates and inspires us the more mythically meaningful our lives become. Without this questioning, we cannot identify the myths that unconsciously possess and misdirect us, nor nurture the ones that will support us in regenerating our wastelands and dying seas.

Storyteller Martin Shaw recognises that the major quests of our time are deeply mythical in nature. He believes that through the process of being broken open by the chaos and crisis of our times, contemporary cultures are leaving behind stories that have toxic consequences.[8] Ecological catastrophes bring us down into the substratum of what really matters. Many emerging myths today tell stories about living with danger, uncertainty and destruction while cultivating love, community and ecological restoration. Often they reference, or have resonance with, traditional Indigenous worldviews which are founded in love and respect for our Earth and heightened awareness of natural processes, while seeking contemporary pathways for survival and redemption.

While we cannot individually concoct new cultural myths to replace old ones, each one of us can develop our own stories, resonant with mythic themes, in response to climate crisis, as Chapter 2 discusses. In his book *The Myth Gap*, Alex Evans explores the power of telling stories which pivot on inspirational mythic themes and actions such as atonement, redemption and restoration for rallying climate action. He writes:

> The most basic and fundamental responsibility for each if us is to make a conscious decision about which myths we adopt, rather than unconsciously allowing them to be chosen for us by the media, people around us, or leaders who play on themes of fear or anger.[9]

Echoing this same idea journalist George Monbiot urges individuals, communities and political movements to counter dominant political narratives which focus on competitiveness, conflict and greed with compelling narratives about restoring and transforming communities by focusing on altruism, kindness and social cooperation.[10] Not only does telling and hearing stories with these mythic themes change perceptions about human capacities and social norms, it also inspires action.

Many of humanity's great mythic stories are about the transformations that can happen when we venture into the unknown, whether it be a thick forest, a barren desert or the belly of a whale. Joseph Campbell observed that such myths often begin with a "call to adventure" which, when answered, leads the protagonist through life challenging encounters, stripping away naiveté and limited beliefs. In these stories, maturity and wisdom grow slowly, as various tests and trials forge compassion, integrity, humility and love.

What might we gain by understanding climate crisis as a call to adventure for a transformative mythic journey? Symbols and metaphors are basic to human consciousness and communication, while myths give meaning and heart for life's tests and transformations. Recognising the threats and losses of global ecological destructions, many of us feel like we have tumbled into the underworld, a place of loss and grief. In the mythic underworld, harsh truths are revealed and former glories turn to ashes, as my recounting of the myth of Inanna in the final chapter of this book illustrates. Underworld myths reveal the implacability of death. Until the unexpected rebirth. Myth reminds us that renewal is born from symbolic death; and a new consciousness forms when old beliefs and identities are stripped away during dark times. It is through facing into loss and suffering that Buddha found enlightenment, the Handless Maiden grew new hands, Parsifal healed the Fisher King and Persephone transformed from naïve daughter to underworld Queen.

Right now, humanity as a species needs to develop myths that support the development of maturity, wisdom and agency to face into the causes and effects of climate disruption and ecological collapse. Without this, our lives and planet will become wastelands, literally and metaphorically. One way that we can give meaning to the potentials and difficulties of climate crisis is by perceiving our responses to it mythically as an initiation, or rite of passage, which works both collectively and individually. In his talks, educator and scientist Duane Elgin asks his audiences what developmental stage they think contemporary human culture is at. The vast majority nominate adolescence, pointing to traits like rebelliousness, irresponsibility, grandiosity, recklessness and desire for excitement, instant gratification and status.[11] There are, of course, many positive traits in adolescence, but when an individual or society becomes stuck in any developmental phase, the more problematic, or pathological aspects become more emphasised. Teenage student climate strikers who call out adult political leaders for their reckless lack of responsibility and maturity in failing to address the climate emergency strike such a strong chord, in part because they ironically highlight inappropriate adolescent behaviour in adult leaders while channelling their own teenage energy into committed action. As student activist Greta Thunberg often comments, "they know they haven't done their homework – but we have."[12]

Developing beyond an immature mindset requires initiatory experiences which develop humility and wisdom, while transforming worldviews from ego-centric to eco-centric, as many student strikers are now experiencing. Psychotherapist Bill Plotkin takes an individual view on this developmental process:

> As soon as enough people in contemporary societies progress beyond adolescence, the entire consumer-driven economy and egocentric life style will implode ... No true adult wants to be a consumer, worker bee, or tycoon, or a soldier in an imperial war.[13]

Proceeding from a collective viewpoint, Elgin pictures waves of ecological calamities, economic crises and civil unrest over time, presenting our species with a non-negotiable lifesaving choice to "discover a common sense of reality, identity and social purpose."[14] In an interconnected and interdependent world, individual and collective can never stray far from one and other. Maturity can only be developed and lived in relationship with other beings, human and otherwise, when it is supported by social systems of education, health governance and justice. Our emergent myths need to drive life-respecting personal and cultural transformations.

Creative mythic visions are already arising in response to the momentousness of this time in world history. Eco-philosopher and campaigner Joanna Macy describes our era as the "Great Turning," a time which presents the need and the opportunity to make the transition "from a doomed economy of industrial growth to a life-sustaining society committed to the recovery of our world."[15] Writer Charles Eisenstein talks about the current dominant global culture living in a mythology of separation, which resorts to war terminology to confront problems. But now, he suggests, initiatory lessons about mutual destruction, such as nuclear weaponry and climate chaos, are sparking a cultural evolution towards a healing "Story of Interbeing."[16] Zen teacher Susan Murphy also sees a mythic call for healing in climate crisis. She suggests Earth is setting us a *koan*, or a kind of spiritual riddle which works to bridge the splits we create in our thinking in order to restore ourselves to an openness of mind. She writes that the climate crisis *koan* not only asks:

> "Where and what is the thinking that did not create the problem?" but also "how can we wrap our minds and hearts around something so vast as the destruction of the biosphere, and instead of going mad, grow alert and interested?"[17]

Framings and namings such as these evoke mythic themes and narratives of developing consciousness about human agency and planetary destiny, the choices that we face and the wisdoms that we need to live by for future survival.

In the midst of rites of passage, feelings of confusion, disorientation, despair and grief inevitably arise as old certainties and securities fall away. We cannot approach our lives with a new vision, until we recognise and abandon prevailing dysfunctional myths and their daily assumptions. Individually and collectively, this is our time in the desert, asking what really matters, and what we must do in order to live well, or indeed live at all. Going into rites of passage, we feel the perilousness of our lives and of all life. Coming through them, we encounter rebirth and renewal, and a strengthened consciousness of, and connection to, Earth and universal processes.

Changing minds

The Buddha taught "With our thoughts we make the world."[18] In order to respond effectively to ecological challenges, we have to change our minds and our way of seeing the world and ourselves. Environmentalist David Suzuki sums it up like this: "So long as we assume that we are the centre of the universe and everything revolves around us, we will not be able to see the dangers we create."[19] Narcissistic desires for self-enhancement and self-gratification are heavily promoted in consumerist societies. The social and ecological consequences of this are becoming ever more apparent as temperatures rise and social equity plummets. The realisation that our world cannot support limitless consumption, is not so much an "an inconvenient truth," as an insistent call to consciousness and systemic change.

The first step towards changing consciousness in response to climate disruption is allowing our ecological destructions to come to mind, and stay there. This is not easy. Resistance to thinking about climate crisis is very high because it arouses deeply disturbing feelings such as fear, powerlessness and grief. Nevertheless ecological dangers are constantly playing around the edges of our minds, inducing ongoing anxieties. Recent research across the UK, US, Canada and Australia showed that 54% of respondents rated the risk of our way of life ending within the next 100 years at 50% or greater, while 24% rated the risk of humans being wiped out at 50% or greater. More encouragingly almost 80% of respondents agreed with the statement that "we need to transform our worldview and way of life if we are to create a better future for the world."[20] It seems that many understand that our present way of living has reached its limits and that we must change how we both think and live to survive the dangers of societal and ecological collapse. The seeds for consciousness change are in the ground. Now is the time to water and fertilise them.

Depth psychology has a focus on expanding consciousness through identifying unconscious aspects of being. It has an adventurous and inquiring approach to the complex and problematic aspects of human psychology and life, encouraging us to question, observe and reflect on unknown or shadowy aspects of ourselves. What we might learn through this process of self-examination is often both revelatory and confronting. Depth psychologist John Gosling writes that psychological growth:

> requires the willingness to suffer more consciously our own humanity, including those aspects we prefer to deny. We are called upon to acknowledge our own assets and limitations, our strengths and our weaknesses. In short, we need to accept our own flawed humanity.[21]

Analysing the psychological terrain of responses (or lack of responses) to climate disruption spells out human weaknesses and strengths in bright lights. As a species we are status-seeking, death-denying, acquisitive and self-absorbed as well as curious, co-operative, empathic and problem solving. These very human characteristics are the basic ingredients we have to work with in addressing how our daily actions, often driven by unconscious assumptions and motivations, are dramatically disrupting Earth's ecosystems. If we can bring these destructive and creative capacities into consciousness and work with them for ecological healing, we can evolve as individuals and societies. Without this evolution, even our most genius technological innovations will crumble into sand.

Changing consciousness is always a bumpy ride. It involves sacrificing protective, and often restrictive and distorting, fantasies about ourselves and the nature of life. We need both support and stamina to negotiate the feelings of fear, guilt, anger and grief which get stirred up along the way. The first seeds of consciousness change sprout when we recognise both the mess we are in, and our fears about changing it. Whether it be addressing a dysfunctional marriage or the climate crisis, this highly unsettling recognition is necessary if we are to make better choices and mature as a species. The opportunities that arise in response to any crisis come about because crisis unseats habitual understandings and behaviour. Acknowledging what no longer works is a necessary spur to look beyond constricting views and situations, and to risk entering unknown and vulnerable places. Usually we take two steps forward and one step back as we inch away from old securities to taste the wild uncertainties of life in the raw.

Consciousness change beckons us into a deeper engagement with ourselves and life, taking us beyond what we know. Humanity celebrates this archetypal journey through art, literature and spiritual narratives, calling upon symbolic language and imagery to express what lies beyond rational thought. Instinct, intuition, imagination and feeling are crucial vehicles for negotiating ourselves and our world, as traditional Indigenous societies well know. In times of crisis, it is particularly helpful to pay heed to dreams, spontaneous images and body sensations as they reveal what our conscious minds censor or fail to apprehend. Carl Jung wrote, when we run into an impasse, dreams can show us "the unvarnished, natural truth" delivering insights which radically alter the attitudes that led us into the impasse.[22] To think outside of the box of rational thought, we have to open up to what sits on the margins of consciousness, or beyond, by paying attention to phenomena that work through other modes of perception including dreams, imaginings and synchronistic events.

Neither consciousness change nor systemic change progresses in a linear fashion, as a consequence of logic. If there is anything that climate change debates have shown us about human nature so far, it is that rational arguments are nowhere sufficient to change minds, let alone consciousness. To see, feel, think and act differently we need to engage with the climate crisis with all of our being: mind, body, heart and soul. Then we can both respect what scientific methods tells us, and be moved by subjective forms of knowing which are attuned to healing possibilities and directions.

One person who understands this well is Jeff Kiehl, a climate scientist who at the age of fifty started studying psychology to gain understanding into the reasons behind climate denial and inaction. His choice to train as a clinician "to understand human behaviour at the most practical level"[23] eventually led to him work as a Jungian analyst in private practice as well as a senior climate scientist at the National Center for Atmospheric Science in the United States. Kiehl is drawn to Jung's depth psychological approach because of the way it illuminates conflicts between conscious thoughts and unconscious processes. Like Jung, he sees value in paying attention to myths, dreams and imagining. Kiehl observes:

> The discussions around finding solutions to the problem of climate change are one-sided in that they predominantly rely on rational thought. Of course, we need to use rational thought processes to look at problems like climate change. However, from a Jungian perspective there are other ways of looking at problems. Jung argued that one-sidedness is the root of neurosis and that we need to balance say the rational with the non-rational. So, to adequately address climate change, we need to use multiple ways of seeing and relating to the world …
>
> For decades psychologists have found that humans process information through two basic pathways. One is linear, verbal and cognitive, which is located in the neocortex region of the brain. The second is affective, imagistic and metaphoric, which is located in the limbic system of the brain … recent findings in neuroscience and decision making research [demonstrate] that the affective part reacts faster than the cognitive part. It means that when I present people with images of climate change they will react affectively to this material, and those affective reactions will occur before any thoughts come to mind and … all of this is happening unconsciously. So, from a purely neuro-scientific perspective we need to consider the unconscious along with the conscious dimensions of psyche when looking at problems like climate change.[24]

Jungian perspectives have been influential in my own life, personally and professionally for the best part of forty years. Like Kiehl, one of the things I appreciate about Jung is his lifelong concern about modern culture's separation from the natural world. Alongside this concern, Jung focuses on the importance of living in conscious relationship with the instinctual and spiritual aspects of human being. Instinctual knowing tells us how to survive, when we are in danger and what to do in response. Spiritual awareness gives meaning, sustenance and inspiration which connects us to both earthy and universal life processes. Both aspects are vital to consider in our engagement with the existential crisis brought about by human-caused climate disruption and ecological collapse.

Full-bodied engagement

Our bodies, like other ecosystems, are highly attuned living systems of intelligence with their own stories. They are vehicles for instinctual and intuitive knowing that our rational minds cannot perceive or apprehend. Making the connection between personal consciousness, bodily experience and the aliveness of Earth releases the mind from scientific reductionism and objectifying views of Earth. Australian author and conservationist Tim Winton suggests:

> Perhaps the simplest and most profound lesson to be learnt from Aboriginal lawmen and women is that the relationship to country is corporeal and familial. We need a more intimate acquaintance with facts. We need to feel them in our bodies and claim them and belong to them as if they were kin.[25]

To nurture ecological consciousness we need to tell stories that draw on this physicality of connection and bring it alive. Uncle Max Harrison is a Yuin elder from the south coast of New South Wales. His advice on how to meet climate disruption starts like this:

> people should be going to sit on land and really understand what they're on, ... and then starting to put some great energy back in, and asking mother earth for forgiveness. I'm definitely sure that they can start restoring some order that way ....
> ... a tree's a good teacher, it can change your mind, sitting under a tree, or feeling the water and that, take your shoes off, and if you stand on the beach with your eyes closed, and feel the wave coming up, and then touching you and going back, and I'm sure that people will be able to feel the heartbeat of the mother, I'm *positively* sure that most people will be able to feel that ...
> And if that goes back out into the ocean ... and if they can follow that connectedness up, then they can start to know what they are taking from there. It'll talk to you, that great expanse of water is telling us things, especially when it gets rough – to me that's Gadu getting angry, saying yous are raping the land underneath me.[26]

Uncle Max's words are for all of us. You do not have to be Indigenous to sit and connect to country through your body and feel into kinship. Whatever your ethnic background, if you go back far enough your Indigenous ancestors await you with their embodied stories about how to relate well to our living Earth. Our new ecological stories about the living systems of Earth have very long roots, as we explore further in Chapter 4.

Stories rooted in somatic processes and ecological consciousness reveal intimate relations between all lives on Earth. The universe is "a communion of subjects rather than a collection of objects" declare Brian Swimme and Thomas Berry in their telling of *The Universe Story*.[27] Their metaphysical vision combines Indigenous knowledge, subjective experience and scientific data to tell a story of life's interconnections. We need stories like theirs which speak to us physically, emotionally and spiritually as well as intellectually to drive radical and fast-moving changes in response to the climate crisis. We also need to speak of our own experiences of ecological destructions in our world, the places we love, the species extinctions we grieve, the heat that disturbs our sleep, the changes in seasons. Climate and ecological disruption is becoming ever more present in our world. Opening to all dimensions of this from physical through to spiritual is essential for full-bodied, whole-hearted responses.

Bringing consciousness to how we live within global ecosystems opens up a larger experience of life. Many of us are in the process of re-imagining ourselves in a wider world with a bigger story. This changes how we see ourselves and how we relate to others. In the words of Linda Cairnes, an activist and artist in my research group, "to embrace the reality of what … is happening, we have to develop other-regarding rather than self-regarding." This isn't an easy or quick process. Many people in contemporary cultures are mired in short-sighted habits entrenched in separatist views of ourselves and our natural world. Nevertheless consciousness change is happening. More and more people are making daily choices based on an awareness of how ecosystems work, whether it be planting native gardens, taking keep cups to cafes or buying organically grown food. Simple caring acts that reflect a systemic view of our place in the world. While far more revolutionary changes than these simple practices are necessary to avoid catastrophic climate chaos, they do speak of growing understandings that are more able to accept this necessity.

A greater sense of connection fosters compassionate responses. Thupten Jinpa, is a Buddhist teacher and translator for the Dalai Lama. In his work as a research psychologist, he also helped to design the Compassion Cultivation Training (CCT) at Stanford University School of Medicine. He writes:

> With a compassionate shift of focus from our own narrow self-agenda (and the heaviness that tends to go with it) to others, we feel lighter. The same stressors may exist in our lives, but we feel less stressed out by them. For what makes our normal response to stress so stressful is how it weighs us down and how we fear it will overwhelm us. Compassion, on the other hand lightens us up. We feel our individual burden lift a little. We see it in perspective. We realize we're not carrying it alone.[28]

This last point is crucial. Global ecological issues, such as the climate crisis and biodiversity loss, are not problems that are caused or solved by any one individual. They are systemic issues that have to be addressed at a collective level. Our role as individuals is to join with others to effect social transformation. While engaging with ecological problems expands personal consciousness in a way that can be healing for both ourselves and our Earth, it is our collective capacities for connection, co-operation, compassion and innovation that are the foundation stones for effective action. Our best and only choices for human surviving and thriving depend on recognising our capacities for collective imagining, learning and action.

One source of inspiration for transformative collective action comes from key points in history when individuals and societies have responded powerfully to enacting new understandings and changing behaviours. Very often the impetus for revolutionary social movements have been inspired by spiritual and ethical visions as well as physical injustices, such as the abolition movement against slavery, the American Civil Rights movement or the Suffragette campaigns. The success of social change movements is traditionally founded upon a critical mass of people who are inspired to attend protests, write letters and books, speak in public meetings, organise strikes and boycotts, and challenge families and colleagues. Today, climate action movements do all this and more, with the added resources of the internet. As a result, communities and cultures across the globe are not only embracing consciousness change and innovative behaviours, they are also answering the call to rise up for climate action. People are buying local, lobbying against single use plastic, installing solar panels, sharing cars and divesting from fossil fuels in increasing numbers. While international and national political action is frustratingly slow and pockets of resistance entrenched, the grassroots momentum for systemic change is building as climate disruption is increasingly experienced as an alarming physical reality, a systemic injustice and an existential crisis of hitherto unknown proportions. We live in sobering times. The challenges are now very clear. Modern societies, and those of us who live within them, must urgently and radically change our ways of perceiving and acting to protect the viability of our own, and many other species. Many of the technologies we need are within reach, but the consciousness and action needed to adopt them on a global scale is dependent on a collective willingness to embrace revolutionary social, political, economic and legal reforms. None of this will proceed without critical conscious change and climate action undertaken by a significant mass of people who can envision and create ecological care and cultural transformation. The revolution we need now is an evolutionary one, driven by ecological pressures, inspired by compassionate dreams and effected through courage and determination. It is already well under way and ramping up, from street protests through to declarations of climate emergency. There is a place for each and every one of us in this revolution, from political campaigns and ecological restoration projects through to community initiatives and daily conversations. As Greta Thunberg told the leaders of the United Nations "change is coming whether you like it or not."[29] Joining with others to make that change as life honouring as possible is the most meaningful step any of us can take in our lives at this watershed moment in human existence.

Notes

1 Bateson, G. Retrieved from www.anecologyofmind.com/reviews.html
2 Jung, C. G. (1977). *The symbolic life* (Collected Works Vol. 18). London, UK: Routledge & Kegan Paul, p. 112.
3 Marshall, G. (2014). *Don't even think about it: Why our brains are wired to ignore climate change*. London, UK: Bloomsbury, p. 19.
4 Kahan, D. M., Wittlin, M., Peters, E., Slovic, P., Ouellette, L. L., Braman, D. & Mandel, G. N. (2011). The tragedy of the risk-perception commons: Culture conflict, rationality conflict, and climate change. *Temple University Legal Studies Research Paper No. 2011–26; Cultural Cognition Project Working Paper No. 89.* Retrieved from http://papers.ssrn.com/sol3/papers.cfm?abstract_id=1871503
5 Campbell, J. (1988). *The power of myth.* New York, NY: Doubleday, p.22.

6 Climate march schoolchildren: "We need change and we need it now." Feb 15 2019 BBC News. Retrieved from www.bbc.com/news/uk-47250424

7 Lear, J. (2006). *Radical hope: Ethics in the face of cultural devastation.* Cambridge, MA: Harvard University Press, p.7.

8 Shaw, M. (2018). Mud and antler bone: An interview with Martin Shaw. *Emergence.* Retrieved from https://emergencemagazine.org/story/mud-and-antler-bone/

9 Evans, A. (2017). *The myth gap: What happens when evidence and arguments aren't enough?* London, UK: Eden Project Books, pp. 105–106.

10 Monbiot, G. (2017, Sept 9). George Monbiot: How do we get out of this mess? *The Guardian.* Retrieved from www.theguardian.com/books/2017/sep/09/george-monbiot-how-de-we-get-out-of-this-mess

11 Elgin, D. (2009). *The living universe: Where are we? Who are we? Where are we going?* San Francisco, CA: Berrett Koehler.

12 Thunberg, G. (2019). *No one is too small to make a difference.* London, UK: Penguin, p. 36.

13 Plotkin, B. (2008). *Nature and the human soul: Cultivating wholeness and community in a fragmented world.* Novato, CA: New World Library, p. 8.

14 Elgin, D. (2009). *The living universe: Where are we? Who are we? Where are we going?* San Francisco, CA: Berrett Koehler, p. 141.

15 Macy, J. & Johnstone, C. (2012). *Active hope: How to face the mess we are in without going crazy.* Novato, CA: New World Library, p. 26.

16 Eisenstein, C. (2018). *Climate: A new story.* Berkeley, CA: North Atlantic Books.

17 Murphy, S. (2012). *Minding the earth, mending the world.* Sydney, Australia: Picador, p. 211.

18 Quoted in Jinpa, T. (2015). *A fearless heart: Why compassion is the key to greater wellbeing.* London, UK: Piatkus, p. 90.

19 Suzuki, D. (2015). *Letters to my grandchildren.* Sydney, Australia: New South, p. 129.

20 Randle, M. & Eckersley, R. (2015). Public perceptions of future threats to humanity and different societal responses: A cross-national study. *Futures.* Retrieved from http://dx.doi.org/10.1016/j.futures.2015.06.004.

21 Gosling, J. (2009). 'Protracted adolescence': Reflections on forces informing the American collective. In S. Porterfield, K. Polette & T. F. Baumlin (Eds.), *Perpetual adolescence: Jungian analyses of American media, literature and pop culture.* Albany, NY: SUNY, p. 143.

22 Jung, C. G. (1964). *Civilisation in transition.* (CW Vol. 10). London, UK: Routledge & Kegan Paul, pp. 149–153.

23 Kiehl, J. T. (2016). *Facing climate change: An integrated path to the future.* New York, NY: Columbia University Press, p. 5.

24 Kiehl, J. T. (2019). Facing climate change through a Jungian lens. In B. Bright & J. P. Marshall (Eds.), *Earth, climate dreams: Dialogues with depth psychologists in the age of the Anthropocene.* Honolulu, HI: Depth Insights, pp. 39–66.

25 Winton, T. (2015). *Island home: A landscape memoir.* London, UK: Hamish Hamilton, p. 229.

26 Murphy, S. (2009). Conversation with Dulumnmun, Uncle Max Harrison. In J. Marshall (Ed.), *Depth psychology, disorder & climate change.* Sydney, Australia: Jung Downunder, pp. 123–124.
27 Swimme, B. & Berry, T. (1994). *The universe story.* New York, NY: Harper Collins, p. 243.
28 Jinpa, T. (2015). *A fearless heart: Why compassion is the key to greater wellbeing.* London, UK: Piatkus, p. 40.
29 Thunberg, G. (2019). *No one is too small to make a difference.* London, UK: Penguin, p. 16.

Chapter 2

Falling off the edge of the known world

Unsettling news

Sometimes we choose to leap off the edge of our known world, other times we are pushed. In today's climate disrupted world, our familiar shores are departing from us. This may not be as apparent in your neighbourhood, as it is for someone living on a Pacific Island or in Bangladesh or Greenland, but global heating is already shifting coastlines, glaciers and seasonal harvests significantly. Our familiar world is fast becoming unfamiliar. There is little choice but to change. One of the best options is to embrace these daunting times as a necessary rite of passage for human consciousness which develops respect, responsibility and reverence for Earth's web of life and our embeddedness within this.

A change of consciousness requires us to cross over emotional and intellectual thresholds. In order to develop ecological consciousness, we must face into our vulnerabilities and deepest fears, as individuals and as a species. This challenge is one that Barbara Kingsolver creatively explores in her novel *Flight Behaviour*. In it, the protagonist, an impoverished rural woman called Dellarobia, befriends a biologist who teaches her about the causes and effects of climate disruption. In response, Dellarobia feels "an entirely new form of panic."[1] She wonders how scientists can bear such knowledge, but then she steadies herself with the thought that people have "to manage terrible truths" in life. Learning to face and manage the panics and terrible truths of life is the path of maturity. Through her novel, Kingsolver shows how Dellarobia expands her consciousness and life direction by engaging with both personal and collective "terrible truths." This is a common theme in many novels, but what is novel about this one is how it focuses on the relationship between developing human consciousness and the growing threats of climate chaos.

Barbara Kingsolver understands that it is an evolutionary advance for humans to make the conscious effort and commitment to learn to face into our fears and panics in the world, rather than to flee them. In an interview about *Flight Behaviour*, she talked about her own struggles to manage the terrible truths of climate change and her feelings of duty to stay engaged with the huge and terrifying questions it brings up because of her own and other children.[2] Letting go of familiar and reassuring views, and facing into fear is deeply unsettling and unnerving. Depth psychologist Robert Romanyshyn recognises that contemporary climate and ecological crises are psychological crises. He writes:

> the melting ice is here with us, lives with us as a sense of anxiety, accompanies us as emotional states of dread and fear, and companions us as a pervasive quality of dis-ease that breaks through an un-nameable irritation like a telephone call in the night that awakens us from sleep.[3]

We cannot help but feel shock and disbelief when we hear news that what seemed unquestioningly secure is at deeply risk. It takes time, repeated tellings and embodied experience for us to maintain consciousness of the losses and threats of our destabilising climate.

Climate information that elicits fear can also readily arouse anger. This became clear to me one night watching a televised climate change debate when one woman's angry denials of the climate scientists' messages morphed into an urgent plea for them to "stop frightening me." She expressed a raw terror that we all feel at the thought of losing basic securities which underpin the lives we have and love. Watching this, I felt my own judgement and anger about her denials dissolve into understanding and empathy. Hearing or reading about climate science and its reports can be very traumatising, sparking a range of responses from paralysis to panic, which are often quickly suppressed. When traumatic responses are not consciously recognised, they can readily fuel a dismissal of climate scientists and their messages. Seeking out reassuring authority figures who will tell us that there is no climate danger, is one way to keep panic at bay. Climate denialist groups and their fossil-fuel funded "experts" recognise and respond to this yearning for reassurance as much as they themselves may be driven by them.

It takes time and a great deal of support to face into daunting realities which threaten our security, especially when, as is often the case with climate disruption, we do not feel or see any immediate danger. Research shows that our brains' hardwiring readily dismisses climate crisis threats because they are "complex, unfamiliar, slow moving, invisible and intergenerational."[4] In other words, they are hard to see, difficult to grasp and too far off. Furthermore, climate disruption threatens our sense of security in many basic ways ranging, from livelihoods through to belief systems.[5] Very often presentations on the climate crisis can become a blur of shocking figures and graphs which induce people to shut down. Sleepiness, boredom and anger can all be protective defences against traumatisation. The climate scientist who talks dispassionately about the evidence can often seem disconnected from the traumatic nature of their message. What often happens then is that the scientist's apparent disconnection feeds the audience's disconnection, while unacknowledged feelings of terror and despair become the elephant in the room, blocking connection and engagement with others.

Fortunately, some climate scientists are becoming more aware that their messages are traumatising and are seeking ways to address this. Jeff Kiehl, the climate scientist and Jungian analyst who we met in the previous chapter, is at the forefront of this work. When he presents the latest scientific understandings to groups of people, he pauses to invite people to speak about their feelings, knowing full well the depth of feeling that this information elicits. He describes one such occasion:

> The moods expressed include sadness, hopelessness, anger, denial, guilt, numbness, and fear. We sit together in silence, holding the multitude of moods. Giving voice to the silent spirits inhabiting our hearts brings a certain warmth to the room. In sharing our feelings about these issues a door opens, connecting us ... Our shared feelings evoke within us a profound depth of caring.[6]

People need to be able to talk freely about these kinds of feelings with one another to help process the complex emotions that climate change awareness triggers. My own experiences in group conversations of sharing responses to climate disruption have been transformative. To be able to express fears, griefs, doubts, despairs and helplessness and listen to others grappling with these same feelings, is deeply relieving and bonding. Typically, people say they feel less alone and more inspired to engage with issues after these conversations. The mind clears, the heart opens and the elephant in the room, once acknowledged, becomes a strength not a hindrance.

When given enough time and space, conversations about how we really feel and think about climate disruption can develop into explorations of profound questions about the nature of the world and ourselves. In my research group, our discussions ranged through questions about death and the afterlife, the relationship between science and spirituality, the effect of belief systems and the role of the imagination, to name but a few. It was both riveting and nurturing to air our fears and delve beneath them. Remarkably, no one in the group dropped out over the course of the year. Perhaps because, as one person put it, our discussions spoke to an "unmet need to be with this." Evening after evening we found we had so much to talk about in conversations that were disturbing, enlivening, sad, thoughtful and at times surprisingly funny. Together we could think beyond where we so often individually faltered, finding support and the freedom to explore thoughts and feelings we would ordinarily keep at bay.

Climate disruption throws up existential questions about the values and viability of our present lives. Both big and unsettling questions, and rich and fruitful ones. When we can resist the urge to back off from what frightens us, we can work out what truly matters and how to respond wisely. In order to do this we need more spaces and opportunities to explore what the climate crisis means to us, and how we feel about it with others. When we have this, we can build strength together to face into a range of deeply challenging issues with compassion, curiosity and creativity. Then we can start to imagine different ways of living on Earth.

Heartening stories

Acknowledging emotions is vital to climate engagement. So too is finding an inviting narrative. The most engaging climate stories are ones that offer inspiration, connections and a creative path of action, along with a truthful assessment of present and future dangers and opportunities. They help us face into the losses and find ways of restoring the world while re-storying our own lives in response to ecological crises and destructions.

In her book *This Changes Everything* Naomi Klein tells the story of how her life changed after a conversation about global warming with Angelica Navarro Llanos, Bolivia's ambassador to the World Trade Organisation, in 2009. Navarro Llanos suggested to Klein that the emergency of climate change could act as a catalyst for positive action on a range of pressing global issues including social justice, income inequity and crumbling public infrastructure. Klein wrote that this conversation was:

> the precise moment when I stopped averting my eyes from the reality of climate change, or at least when I first allowed my eyes to rest there for a good while ... After this conversation I found that I no longer feared immersing myself in the scientific reality of the climate threat. I stopped avoiding the articles and the scientific studies ... I also stopped outsourcing the problem to the environmentalists, stopped telling myself this was somebody else's issue, somebody else's job.[7]

Klein read widely and talked with climate justice activists. She developed her own vision of a global mass movement that could act to protect humanity from "the ravages of both a savagely unjust economic system and a destabilised climate system."[8] Since then, Klein has become a powerful advocate for climate justice movements. The story she tells through her campaigns is that the climate crisis is delivering a fiery message about our need to evolve new patterns of sharing our planet and its resources. Her story has a motivating narrative which identifies the problems, the actions needed in response, and a vision of what can be created out of the crisis through collective global action.

While this is not the only possible narrative, these are the kinds of narratives we need more of to overcome the considerable resistances to climate action that operate at individual and collective levels. Klein's comment about averting her eyes and avoiding scientific data prior to her change of viewpoint, describes how many people respond to climate reports, much of the time. There are a number of reasons for this, some conscious, others unconscious. Over the years I have had many discussions with people who have told me that they don't think too much about climate change because there is "nothing we can do" or because "it makes me too anxious," or that "smart technology will sort it out" or that global warming is "not so bad," "not proven" or "not going to affect me in my lifetime." The only comments that I don't hear about climate change is that "I have never heard of it," or "I have no opinion about it." By now, everyone has shaping stories about climate disruption, and their relation towards it, whether they be ones that avoid or promote engagement. Not infrequently, contradictory narratives fight it out within ourselves as well as in the world. It is often only when we can talk it out and work it through, preferably in the company of others, that we can find some kind of conscious consistent viewpoint that supports response and action.

To break the paralysing bind of averting our eyes from the climate crisis, we need to find ways of naming and working through the conflicts and upsetting emotions that it brings to consciousness, such as guilt, anxiety, grief and hopelessness. Full engagement with climate issues requires acknowledging the destructive consequences of fossil-fuel use, land clearing practices and industrialised farming practices, as well as love and respect for, and dependence upon, our planet. In Western culture there has been an entrenched background story, based on beliefs about the "rightness" of human dominion over Earth, along with an assumption that Earth has an infinite capacity to sustain human activities of any kind. This myth is failing the reality test of climate disruption and ecological collapse. The consequences of holding on to it are clearly catastrophic. Relinquishing it opens up the space for new stories that acknowledge the complexity and boundaries of ecosystems, and the ways we can live within them.

Eshana Bragg is an ecopsychologist who explores the consequences of the narratives we use to make sense of our world. She writes "The stories we tell ourselves at this point in history will not only affect our psychological health but profoundly affect our planetary health and survival as a species."[9] Bragg tells the story of a spontaneous shift she had in her own perception about climate change while sitting on her local beach in the aftermath of an unusually ferocious storm. She started thinking about how storms are nature's way of redistributing the mounting heat-energy in Earth's atmosphere. A hurricane that we call a natural disaster, Bragg realised, could equally well be understood as a natural mechanism which works towards maintaining climatic equilibrium. From this moment on, Bragg began to see climate disruption as an "ally" that both challenges our destructive human behaviours within our planetary ecosystem, and invites us to rethink what matters most in life. Through this lens, she can understand the damaging effect human activity has on climatic conditions alongside nature's propensity to address imbalances and support life. Bragg's heartening story revisions our relationship with our natural world, empowering us to become conscious collaborators with Earth's healing processes, rather than victims or villains.

Stories of transition help us to navigate our lives within new found currents. They stretch our worlds, imaginations and identities, by requiring us to examine our beliefs, values, behaviours and conflicts in the light of newly emerging circumstances. No one story is right or wrong, but the most empowering face into challenges while giving meaning and purpose in their negotiation. Many stories are emerging at present in relation to ecological disruptions and pressures. The best inspire creative strategies and restorative practices, while acknowledging the risks and uncertainties ahead. Their effect on us is very different to another form of futuristic story, frequently aired in response to climate crisis, which anticipates apocalyptic finalities, rather than transitions of varying degrees of difficulties.

Imagining the worst

Apocalyptic fantasies have always had a place in the human imagination, fuelling a steady supply of prophecies about the "end of the world." These days, apocalyptic stories are being dished up with a fresh twist, featuring rising sea levels, superstorms, droughts, wildfires, ocean acidification, and tipping points. The scenarios are contemporary, but the way they are being told by some is worryingly familiar. All too often climate change scenarios are being hijacked by apocalyptic narratives that breed fatalistic and/or panicked responses. The dangers of climate disruption are real enough; however, at times the imagined outcomes can run along well-trod tracks, which reflect more about ourselves, our state of mind and our myths than changes in our world.

If you are my age, you will be familiar with many doom-laden prophecies, from the so-called end of the Mayan calendar through to those associated with nuclear winter, the Y2K bug or peak oil scenarios. As yet, none of these has eventuated, although oil shortages, computer hacks or failures and nuclear contamination are all problematic features of modern life which can have tragic consequences if not taken seriously. The dangers are very real when not addressed, but the apocalyptic narratives of collapse imagined around them have as much to do with existential feelings of vulnerability, insecurity and uncertainty, as they do about the way we live in the thrall of technology.

Throughout human history and across many societies, people have told and believed doomsday tales, especially during times of major change. Such stories have mythic roots and archetypal themes. Typically they recount or prophesy the end of times, often as a consequence of humanity's sins. Some myths tell of past cataclysmic events, like Noah's Flood in the Bible. Others, such as the Christian Rapture or the Islamic Last Judgement anticipate future ones. Their details vary across different times and cultures, but the underlying themes are similar in pattern.

Universally, mythic stories are preoccupied with existential themes of life, death and renewal. Apocalyptic myths in particular grapple with the inevitability of loss and mortality in our lives and world. We hear them most when our societies and environments are under threat. In the second half of the twentieth century, our collective apocalyptic imaginings started to grapple with the enormity of damage inflicted on Earth by humans. Nuclear holocaust, mutant superbugs and climate chaos all began to feature in end of the world imaginings, as the consequences of our collective actions became more terrifying to us than the wrath of gods.

In recent years climate fears in particular are fuelling a growing genre of apocalyptic films and novels which feature flooded countries, scorching deserts and scarce resources. Dystopian fantasies ranging from the political, such as Margaret Atwood's *Oryx and Crake* trilogy, through to action thrillers, like *The Maze Runner* series can raise awareness of global ecological destructions and the high stakes of not addressing them. But they also run the risk of creating self-fulfilling prophecies of social and ecological collapse by fuelling feelings of fatalistic despair.

Catastrophic thinking thrives when we exaggerate the forces against us and underestimate our own resources.[10] Which is one good reason not to fixate on bad news stories. As climate campaigner Bill McKibben wryly observes:

> The trouble with obsessing over collapse … is that it keeps you from considering other possibilities. Either you've got your fingers stuck firmly in your ears, or you're down in the basement oiling your guns. There's no real room for creative thinking.[11]

I agree. Our focus needs to be on our strengths and strategies for facilitating personal and social changes that can both mitigate and adapt to climate disruption as best we can. Nevertheless I do think we need to consciously acknowledge the universal and ongoing presence of apocalyptic myths and the effects of their catastrophic fears in order not to be held hostage by them.

In the early meetings of our research group, apocalyptic talk and imaginings frequently surfaced. Most of us were not anticipating such dreadful scenarios to unfold, nevertheless we felt compelled to discuss them. Airing our direst fantasies seemed to be a way of acknowledging that we are in a time of climate emergency and the intense feelings of vulnerability, powerlessness and grief that this awareness triggered in us.

I recall one edgy and occasionally raucous conversation about what we might eat if food ran out. We began by asking if the vegetarians amongst us would start eating animals, and ended up pondering how many of us would eat human remains. We concluded that we simply could not know. No amount of fantasising could tell us who we would be, or what we would do, in extreme circumstances way beyond our present lives. Climate disruption signals the end of our familiar world, and with that comes the potential loss of our familiar selves. Climate chaos scenarios haunt us because they pose challenging questions about survival, the nature of humanity, the meaning of life, death and renewal. These are questions that can open vistas, rather than close options. In a time when old myths and ways of living are proving to be non-viable, questions about what makes life worth living and how to understand our place in the world are vital ones that need to be answered in the light of ecological destructions and emerging understandings.

Viewing apocalyptic anxieties through a symbolic lens changes the focus. Literal fears about the end of the world recede while possibilities for consciousness change are highlighted. Psychologists and mythologists recognise that apocalyptic imaginings and dreams often surface when we are on the cusp of an expansion of consciousness. The word apocalypse comes from the Greek word *apokalypsis* which means revelation or the tearing away of a veil. This meaning suggests that our vision increases when old worlds, and the assumptions that informed them, crumble away. Certainly the apocalyptic dream I discussed in Chapter 1, was both a revelation and a wake-up call for me. I saw more of the world and its predicament and, as a consequence, I changed how I viewed myself and my life direction. Crucially, I understood that this dream was an experience of awakening consciousness about the world and my place within it, not a literal prophecy.

Identifying apocalyptic thoughts as *imaginings*, rather than as necessarily real *about to happen* scenarios, was also an important step in our research group discussions. Once we acknowledged this fantasy element, we were more able to share our feelings in response to present climate disasters. We could recognise that rather than fearing the end of the world, we were fearing the end of familiar ways of being, living and thinking. We noticed that after exploring our apocalyptic fantasies, we spontaneously moved into discussions about the here and now, how we felt and what we could do to restore ecosystems and protect ongoing life.

When we move beyond the unconscious sway of apocalyptic fears and fantasies we can address specific present and future dangers, as well as our own underlying emotional states. This frees up the imagination for more lively and creative ways of relating to today's world. For some, this shift is catalysed by becoming involved with initiatives that acknowledge the dangers while envisioning alternatives. Naomi Klein wrote that her immersion with the climate justice movement "helped me imagine various futures that were decidedly less bleak than the post-apocalyptic cli fi pastiche that had become my unconscious default."[12] For others, resilience comes from feeling adequately resourced to meet the challenges of changing climates. Gleb Raygorodetsky, a conservation biologist who works with Indigenous communities reports that, despite the hardships that the climate crisis is already bringing to many Indigenous communities, there "is no sense of doom and gloom."[13] Instead there is a well-tested resilience grounded in their traditional knowledge of working intimately with changing ecological conditions over millennia.

These days I am no longer stalked by apocalyptic imaginings or dreams in the ways that I once was, although I am even more concerned about climate disruption and its consequences. I have learned to accept that I cannot be sure of any scenario ahead, although I do anticipate immense change. This acceptance enables me to hold a conscious resolve to stay open to the world as it is, beautiful and wounded, while doing what I can to contribute to ecological restoration, climate action and cultural change. While grief and anxiety ebbs and wanes in me, so too does hope and inspiration, grounded in the resilience and creativity of the natural world, including human nature.

Facing into fear

Anxiety has always been a part of the human condition. In manageable levels it motivates us to act for our survival. When unmanaged, it can immobilise us. Anxiety's roots lie in the real awareness that what we cherish most – our lives, our loved ones, our homes – can be lost at any time. Climate crisis and biodiversity loss ramps up this existential anxiety. Shifting shorelines, dwindling species, spreading deserts and increasing numbers of refugees are all part of today's overheating world. Anxiety and fear are healthy and necessary responses, especially when the climate emergency is not being fully acknowledged, let alone dealt with, at a political level. It is a significant psychological challenge to negotiate these fears without becoming overwhelmed by them. Nevertheless this challenge can be met in ways that develop resilience and maturity, feeding a strength more able to endure all of life's adversities.

Whenever we do not consciously acknowledge and address our fears, unconscious responses prevail. Psychoanalysts describe an array of defence mechanisms that can come into play when people feel unable to deal with real or imagined threats to the basic securities of life. These are irrational and unconscious responses that seek quick comforting fixes, in place of facing into hard realities. The roots of our psychological defence mechanisms reach back to early childhood, when experiences of powerlessness and confusion are common. Frequently young children seek refuge by telling themselves comforting stories in response to threatening situations and people. Stories like "I have magic powers," "my friend is naughty, not me" or "you will always be here to look after me." Such stories kept anxieties and fears at bay by denying unpleasant truths. While most of us generally outgrow these fantastical denials as we mature and find more resilient ways of meeting our anxieties, more sophisticated denial mechanisms can surface at any age when basic securities come under threat. Often this is part of the process of coming to terms with hard to bear realities, such as life threatening illnesses, divorce or bereavement. In many instances, denial can be a beginning point for learning to negotiate threats and losses. However, there are no guarantees of this. Time, support and internal and external resources are all crucial factors in making the move from denial to acceptance.

Not surprisingly, climate disruption sparks many unconscious defensive mechanisms. These responses often take the form of dogmatic and simplistic beliefs. Some of the more common ones include: denying ("the planet is actually cooling"), disavowing ("warmer weather will be better for us"), minimising ("the situation isn't that bad"), distancing ("well it's not a problem I need to worry about at my age"), fatalising ("there is nothing I can do") blaming or scapegoating ("it's all the fault of those stupid deniers"), projecting fears on to others ("those panic stricken Greenies"), disassociating ("my mind wanders off whenever I hear about climate change") or inflating ("with our technological brilliance we can outsmart any threats"). These deflecting stories seek comfort in the face of the complex and challenging realities of climate change. At best they can give us time to come to terms with "the unthinkable." At worst they escalate unconscious fears in individuals and societies, while leaving us exposed to unaddressed dangers.

Sally Weintrobe is a psychoanalyst who has explored the difference between climate change negation and disavowal.[14] In her view, *negation* is an outright denial of the reality of climate change. It works as an unconscious strategy to buy time to come to terms with the painful truths of global warming. Often, with the right support, it gives way to acceptance. *Disavowal*, however, Weintrobe suggests, is a more entrenched way of distorting climate change realities. Its strategy is to accept that climate disruption is happening while at the same time minimising and muddling the issues. Disavowal can be both conscious and unconscious in its ongoing sidestepping of outer and inner conflicts provoked by climate change. It is widespread in neoliberal politics with its primary allegiances to fossil fuel economies and unfettered economic growth. While some politicians take refuge in denial, many more live in disavowal, shaping climate policies which appear to address the issue, but in fact avoid dealing with the fundamental causes of rising temperatures. A culture and language of disavowal around climate disruption then becomes normalised, as it has done in Australia, where clean energy is regularly touted as a goal even while new coal mines are encouraged and subsidised.

Ongoing avoidance of hard truths undermines strength, ingenuity and maturity. Twisting away from "what is" through entrenched disavowal, weakens and deforms individuals and societies. The way to break this Catch 22 situation, is to generate both internal and external support and resources to challenge disavowal by calling out its contradictions while providing consistent and empowering narratives that address climate and ecological destructions. A conscious naming and exploration of the anxieties and risks of the climate crisis is crucially important in loosening the deadlock of disavowal. When fears are made conscious and shared, thinking clears and strategies can be developed to monitor and negotiate anxiety levels, for individuals and societies.

Climate chaos fears and risks are increasingly being articulated publicly, most notably by climate campaigners and scientists. These are the people who end up carrying the burden of knowledge and fear for the community at large. For them, living with the daily consciousness of the costs and risks of climate chaos and negotiating the fears that come with this awareness is a part of their lives. Living with climate fear is neither a static nor a dead end process. Psychological research shows that ongoing exposure to what makes us anxious can lead to a lessening of anxiety levels, as we familiarise ourselves with what frightens us. Such a process can be enabling, supporting a more reasoned and active response as anxiety levels lessen.

In a recent radio program on the emotional states of climate scientists, journalist Gretchen Miller reported that when she heard Andrew King, a marine scientist, talk about the near certainty of the Great Barrier Reef dying in the next twenty years, she had a weird sinking anxious feeling in her chest.[15] When Miller asked King "Do you wake in the night?" he responded "To be honest I think I have got used it. It's one of those things you learn over time, and you gradually realise more and more." Listening to this programme the first time, I felt shaky with anxiety as well as overwhelmed by grief. Re-listening to it several months later, the shock was gone and my anxiety was less marked, although my grief was still powerful. The emotional process of familiarising ourselves with news of climate destructions is ongoing. Time and repeated exposure can help us to integrate the realities of climate disruption. When this happens, climate anxiety does not so much disappear as become part of the landscape of our lives and our relationship to the world, which we can reflect upon and integrate over time.

This process of normalising and integrating climate anxiety is the antidote for pervasive feelings of numbness or apathy in response to the climate crisis and biodiversity collapse. Renee Lertzman found that apparent apathy commonly masked strong feelings of anxiety, despair and/or grief, when she conducted research in communities suffering from ongoing environmental degradation.[16] She suggests that lack of environmental engagement may not be because people do not care, but because they care so much. When environmental anxiety, loss or grief is not consciously recognised and negotiated, it fuels an ongoing defence strategy of distancing from the problem which not only compounds the problem but also feeds persistent feelings of melancholia or even depression. This then becomes a force for inaction. To become response-able and engaged, we need to identify, discuss and digest our fears and sadness about ecological losses both individually and within our communities. Creative artists, community workers, educators, campaigners and the helping professions all have an important role in supporting this process.

The trajectory of consciously negotiating climate anxiety and despair is described in Paul Hoggett and Rosmary Randall's research into the emotional resilience of climate campaigners and climate scientists.[17] This research found that climate scientists and campaigners typically went through an initial phase of immersion in climate issues which was frequently accompanied by strong feelings of anxiety, overwhelm and despair. Over time, however, these feelings diminished as people developed "creative and realistic strategies" to manage the psychological challenges of their climate crisis awareness. These included cultivating supportive relationships and groups, positive thoughts and actions, inspirational and achievable projects for a better future, self-care regimes and learning to monitor the amount of time spent reading about and responding to the climate crisis.

When we deny climate anxiety, we restrict our lives, our world-views and our capacity to care. Facing into our fears, learning to share, process, integrate and act on them, builds strength and resources to sustain engagement. In summarising their research into the emotional resilience of climate campaigners and scientists (further discussed in Chapter 6), Hoggett and Randall wrote that "What was striking about our respondents ... was the extent of their maturity and creativity in dealing with difficult situations and with painful emotions."[18] Through sustained engagement, those on the climate front line can develop personally in ways that stand themselves in good stead for responding well to whatever life brings. This is heartening news for us all. It teaches us that bringing conscious attention to our fears, while calling upon supportive resources, makes us stronger and more creative – as we need to be in a world of climate crisis and ecological collapse.

Talking openly

Developing safe and effective ways to address hard realities and contain collective anxieties is particularly crucial at a grassroots level, given the widespread absence of political leadership on the climate crisis. Climate campaigners, scientists, communicators and journalists are all tussling with how to listen to or deliver news of serious human-driven climate disruptions so that it arouses minimum defensiveness and maximum action. After surveying a range of research and communication initiatives, George Marshall advocates adopting a range of approaches, "with different communicators speaking in different ways to different audiences."[19] His pragmatic approach recognises the varying degrees of emotional robustness in particular audiences, as well as the different worldviews and values in play.

Climate communicators need to create a safe space for compassionately acknowledging the depth and range of emotional responses in their audiences, while tailoring storylines that neither falsely reassure, nor counterproductively provoke. Finding out what inspires audiences, and shapes narratives that reinforce people's desires and abilities to act, counterbalances anxieties and resistance, as we explore further in Chapter 6. Particularly crucial is linking individual responses to collective movements and resources, in a way that values and empowers each person's input while validating the support of community. Writing about his own bouts of paralysing anxiety, climate scientist Peter Kalmus reports:

> Things do feel somewhat different now, both because more people are calling for action than in 2006 and also because I'm now part of communities with people who are as concerned as I am (for example, my local chapter of Citizens' Climate Lobby). There are more people in my life talking openly about climate change. And that helps.[20]

We all negotiate our anxieties better when we know we are not alone in having them or in developing effective ways to respond to them.

Renee Lertzman is a consultant in the field of climate communications and psychology. She observes how frequently the emotional and experiential, or *affective* dimensions of climate communications are not made conscious. She suggests that:

> A better approach is to acknowledge affect, have compassion, and work with it. One strategy is to incorporate what Buddhists call "skillful means" into how we negotiate these difficult and complicated feelings and emotions. What this looks like is meeting people where we are; when we recognize, acknowledge and "hold" potential anxieties, it has the direct effect of disarming and softening our tendencies to defend and distance.[21]

Lertzman also suggests that when speaking about climate issues it is important to check in with how you feel yourself, and then share this with others. This can encourage others to identify and share their feelings, while steadying your own emotional responses. The more elephants in the room that are named, the more alive the conversation becomes. Another approach that Lertzman suggests is to be curious and ask questions, like "what worries you most?" and "have you noticed how you handle your anxiety when climate issues crop up?" Responses are rarely one-dimensional. Behind one feeling can be other feelings, as well as the thoughts and beliefs that drive these feelings. One good example of making affects conscious is Jeff Kiehl's invitation to his audience to share how they are feeling in response to his climate science presentations, described earlier in this chapter. Having done this practice many times, Kiehl observes that people do not always know how they are feeling until they are asked.[22]

There are many reasons for the suppression of emotional responses to climate crisis, both cultural and personal. In the public domain in many techno-industrial cultures, cultural taboos steer conversations away from expressing strong emotions, especially those that stir up feelings of vulnerability in either the speaker or the audience. Prevailing worldviews in these cultures also demand a separation of "objective facts" and "subjective responses," with the former being seen as valid and truthful while the latter is often sidelined as confusing or irrelevant.[23]

From a psychological perspective the notion of attempting to separate objective understanding from subjective understanding is deeply problematic, as it can morph into a form of *splitting* or *distancing* that separates thinking from feeling. When this happens, a person can know a situation but not feel it, hindering their ability to respond fully or effectively. In relation to climate disruption, many people recognise the problem "as a fact," but emotionally disconnect in culturally sanctioned ways that significantly weaken overall response. Climate scientists and journalists particularly have to grapple with this cultural split as they are routinely expected to discount their emotional and instinctual responses to what they are researching and reporting. The psychological toll for this suppression is significant, individually and collectively.

Climate discussions have been routinely structured to render a maelstrom of feelings unconscious. Reflecting back on his five years of experience covering climate issues as an environmental reporter, Michael Slezak realised that he had been maintaining a wall between the objective facts and his emotional responses to them. While he understood all the ins and outs of the climate crisis, he felt little of the dread or fear that was appropriate, given what he knew.[24]

Consciously recognising and naming emotional disconnection is crucial in addressing it. For Slezak, it took a number of personal changes to break through his numbness. One change was approaching fatherhood. Another was reading James Bradley's novel *Clade*, which portrays ordinary people in daily family situations dealing with slowly deteriorating environmental conditions due to climate disruption.

What Slezak experienced as his numbness wore off was a form of panic as well as an emotional awakening in himself which while unpleasant also brought relief. Following this, his lack of emotional response to climate issues transformed into a renewed passion to fight for future generations. Slezak found his way out of his emotional numbness through making a more intense connection to the preciousness of life. For him, literature and fatherhood intensified his feeling life, helping to break the spell of a cultural enchantment that favours emotional splitting. Writing about all of this as a journalist was a powerful and revolutionary act, reclaiming personal ground, while challenging a cultural taboo which is having tragic consequences.[25]

Michael Slezak's story illustrates a disconnection that I believe many of us struggle with, both in the way climate change news is presented to us, as well as how we receive it. This needs to be recognised and addressed at all levels of climate communications and discussion. We need to feel grief and fear in the face of looming disasters. They are realistic and motivating emotions. As is learning how to consciously manage them so that we can fully respond. When we can voice our fears and listen respectfully to others' fears, we generally feel less isolated and overwhelmed by them. The validation of what we feel along with empathic support makes what seem unbearable, bearable – and then actionable. When we do consciously engage with our fear, we are more likely to express it, connect with others and act for what is most precious to ourselves and our lives.

Accepting uncertainty

Letting go of our habitual beliefs and expectations about climate and our natural world is a profoundly unsettling and necessary process. The atmosphere, the oceans and the seasons are less fixed and less well understood than many have assumed. Learning from climate scientists that our Earth is warming and that humans are the major cause of this warming undermines so many basic assumptions about how we live, and where we live. Recent research into deep-time geologic records definitively shows that atmospheric CO_2 is a major driver of Earth's climate, and that CO_2 levels are rising more rapidly now than in other geologic periods, even before human times.[26] With increasing CO_2 levels comes ice melt, sea level rises and high rainfall events.[27] Without a doubt, our planet is swiftly changing. What is not so certain is just how these changes will impact our own lives and communities, or if our societies can enact sufficient healing measures to protect continuing life for our species and many others. This uncertainty haunts us and daunts us. Little wonder that many people attempt to cling to opinions and approaches that assume certainty and security, despite mounting evidence to the contrary.

A profound quandary arises when we encounter the unknown and unpredictable in life. We feel stripped of expertise and beliefs just when we feel most in need of something steady to hold on to. Unforeseen events and complexities test prevailing myths and world-views. When they fail the test, many flail. But for those who can consciously accept that we are in a time of great uncertainty riven with many unknowns, this can also be a favourable time for learning, opportunity and creativity.

I wrote the first draft of this chapter in the wake of the election of Donald Trump as the US President. The unexpected outcome of the election combined with the impulsive and erratic nature of Trump's personality and policymaking triggered a massive dose of uncertainty and unease in me, and in pretty well everyone else I knew. My American friends reeled as they grappled with the knowledge that the country they thought they lived in, is not the one they now found themselves in. Many felt very uncertain about what to think or do in response to such an unexpected turn of events, and such a wide reaching change of governmental policies. The ground of habitual assumptions and expectations gave way. The media was alive with debate. Antennas were on high alert, and people started taking notice of happenings in the world way more than usual.

While many people shored up their customary views, others responded to the uncertainty of this turn of events by asking "What is happening? What have I not seen? Where are we heading? What should I do now?" These are productive questions. Whenever we are jolted out of our expectations, there is an opportunity for understanding ourselves, others and our communities beyond the limitations of old assumptions. I was heartened by the author Aleksander Hemon's response to these times when he wrote "Love the new frequencies; what is noise now will be music later. The disintegration of the known world provides a lot of pieces to play with and use in constructing alternatives."[28] Several years into Trump's Presidency, it is true that alternatives are being constructed out of the shambles and destructions being brought about by his administration. Like the action of the majority of the US states and cities who are enacting climate action policies in the absence of Federal commitment, or the emergence of the radical Green New Deal in the lead up to the 2020 elections. Pursuing alternatives like these does not deny or negate the losses and griefs brought out by the decimation of climate action and environmental protections under Trump's administration, but they do bear testimony to how human societies can and do evolve through disruption and tragedy.

In today's complex and unstable world it is more pressing for us to embrace uncertainty than at any other time in human history, writes social scientist Helga Nowotny.[29] Staying on the edge of the unknown is essential for creative breakthroughs, she reminds us. Knowing what we don't know heightens observation, imagination and experimentation. The poet, John Keats, urged an approach to the world which could stay with uncertainties, mysteries and doubts, "without any irritable reaching after fact & reason."[30] For Keats, this attitude, which he called "negative capability," was the basis for creative vision. For us today, it is a way of being that can help us to open our minds and hearts and respond well to the world's rapid and unprecedented changes. It also fosters humility in relationship to the complexities of Earth which will always dwell beyond certainties. Facts and reason have their place; but for us to use them well we need to cultivate the psychological resilience to be able to sit with the uncertainty of things, and of outcomes. Zen Buddhist philosophy teaches the value of the *don't know mind*. When we can be open to what we don't know instead of being filled with the certainty of received knowledge, it brings us alive, keenly observant to what is here rather than blinkered by what we think we know.

Many innovative and effective climate strategies are based upon open-minded observation and experimentation. In her travels around the world exploring climate initiatives, science journalist Gaia Vince observed many inventive projects born out of the uncertainty of changing conditions.[31] One of them was in Ladakh, where she met Chewang Norphel, a retired engineer. Across Ladakh, the future of villages is looking very uncertain as glaciers are retreating and streams are disappearing, leading to failed crops and an outbreak of water disputes. Villagers asked Norphel for help bringing them water, but he had no solutions to offer. Then one winter's day he noticed water gushing from a tap which had been left open in order to stop the pipe from freezing. He told Vince:

> I noticed that on its route to the stream, the water crossed a small wooded field, where it was collecting in pools. Where the trees provided shade, it was freezing into ice patches.[32]

Norphel realised that if he could find a way to replicate this on a large scale he could create an artificial glacier that would melt in spring in time for crop sowing.

Despite ridicule and his lack of modern equipment, Norphel succeeded in constructing a series of glaciers by diverting winter waste water across shaded stone embankments. When the sun rises higher in spring, the glaciers melt providing millions of gallons of water for irrigation canals and aquifers. As a result, land cultivation and tree planting is on the rise. Now neighbouring countries are looking into adopting Norphel's methods for artificial glacier cultivation. This story is just one of many told by Vince as she encountered people across the planet who had come up with ingenious inventions in response to the uncertain and unpredictable conditions created by climate disruption.

Creative responses arise from spending time with what is, rather than what was or what should be. They begin with open-mindedness and the blank canvas of not knowing, and proceed with close attention, moment by moment, step by step. In a time when our planet is entering into climatic conditions unlike those ever known to humanity, we need to embrace uncertainty as a starting point for negotiating a viable future. Our only real certainty is that human life cannot be lived as it has been in these last centuries. The Earth that we thought we knew has already disintegrated to reveal an Earth that we are struggling to recognise and understand. If we can observe well and respect the uncertainties of Earth, we may find, threaded through the dangers, opportunities to explore and learn from our new world, to craft a wiser, humbler and more sustainable way of living.

Notes

1 Kingsolver, B. (2012). *Flight behaviour*. London, UK: Faber & Faber, p. 247.
2 Walsh, B. (2012, Nov 8). Barbara Kingsolver on *Flight Behavior* and why climate change is part of her story. Retrieved from http://entertain ment.time.com/2012/11/08/barbara-kingsolver-on-flight-behavior-climate -change-and-the-end-of-doubt/

3 Romanyshyn, R. D. (2008). The melting of the polar ice: Revisiting Technology as symptom and dream. *Spring: A Journal of Archetype and Culture 80* (Fall 2008), p. 84.

4 Marshall, G. (2014). *Don't even think about it: Why our brains are wired to ignore climate change.* New York, NY: Bloomsbury, p. 226.

5 For a comprehensive review of psychology climate denial see Stoknes, P. E. (2015). *What we think about when we try not to think about global warming.* White River Junction, VT: Chelsea Green.

6 Kiehl, J. T. (2016). *Facing climate change: An integrated path to the future.* New York, NY: Columbia University Press, p. 29.

7 Klein, N. (2014). *This changes everything: Capitalism vs. climate.* New York, NY: Simon & Schuster, p. 7.

8 Ibid, p. 8.

9 Bragg, E. (2015). Climate change as ally. *Ecopsychology 7* (4), 232.

10 Hoggett, P. (2011). Climate change and the apocalyptic imagination. *Psychoanalysis, Culture & Society 16* (3), 11.

11 McKibben, B. (2010). *Eaarth: Making a life on a tough new planet* Melbourne, Australia: Black Inc., p. 99.

12 Klein, N. (2014). *This changes everything: Capitalism vs. climate.* New York, NY: Simon & Schuster, p. 420.

13 Robbins, J. (2018). Native knowledge: What ecologists are learning from Indigenous people. Retrieved from https://e360.yale.edu/features/native-knowledge-what-ecologists-are-learning-from-indigenous-people.

14 Weintrobe, S. (2013). Introduction. In S. Weintrobe (Ed.), *Engaging with climate change: Psychoanalytic and interdisciplinary perspectives.* Hove, UK: Routledge, pp. 7–9.

15 Miller, G. (2016, Oct 31). Climate of despair. *Earshot*, Radio National, ABC Radio. Retrieved from www.abc.net.au/radionational/programs/ear shot/climate-of-emotion:-despair/7880378.

16 Lertzman, R. (2013). The myth of apathy. In S. Weintrobe (Ed.), *Engaging with climate change: Psychoanalytic and interdisciplinary perspectives.* Hove, UK: Routledge, pp. 117–133.

17 Hoggett, P. & Randall, R. Outriders of the coming adversity: How climate activists and climate scientists keep going. Retrieved from www .climatepsychologyalliance.org/explorations/blogs/173-outriders-of-the-coming-adversity-how-climate-activists-and-climate-scientists-keep-going.

18 Ibid.

19 Marshall, G. (2014). *Don't even think about it: Why our brains are wired to ignore climate change.* New York, NY: Bloomsbury, p. 143.

20 Kalmus, P. (2018, Aug 9). The best medicine for my climate grief. Retrieved from www.yesmagazine.org/mental-health/the-best-medicine-for-my-climate-grief-20180809.

21 Lertzman, R. (2014, Mar 12). Breaking the climate fear taboo. Retrieved from www.sightline.org/2014/03/12/breaking-the-climate-fear-taboo/.

22 Kiehl, J. T (2019) Facing climate change through a Jungian lens. In B. Bright & J. P. Marshall (Eds.), *Earth, climate dreams: Dialogues with depth psychologists in the age of the Anthropocene.* Honolulu, HI: Depth Insights, pp. 39–66.

23 It could be well argued that the techno-industrial societies that are driving the climate crisis are the very ones that are most numb to its consequences because of their cultural forms of splitting mind from body, nature from human and emotion from intellect. The blindness that drives ecological destructions, also prevents the witnessing of emotional responses to this.
24 Slezak, M. (2017, Jan 20) Writing about climate change: My professional detachment has finally turned to panic. Retrieved from www.theguardian.com/environment/commentisfree/2017/jan/20/writing-about-climate-change-my-professional-detachment-has-finally-turned-to-panic?CMP=share_btn_fb.
25 Ibid.
26 Kiehl, J. T. (2019, Jun 19). Data from Earth's past holds a warning for our future under climate change. Yale Climate Connections. Retrieved from www.yaleclimateconnections.org/2019/06/data-from-earths-past-holds-a-warning-for-our-future-under-climate-change/.
27 Ibid.
28 Hemon, A. (2017, Jan 17). Stop making sense, or how to write in the age of Trump. Retrieved from www.villagevoice.com/arts/stop-making-sense-or-how-to-write-in-the-age-of-trump-9575300
29 Nowotny, H. (2016). *The cunning of uncertainty.* Cambridge, UK: Polity.
30 Keats, J. (2009, Oct 13). Selection from Keat's letters. Retrieved from www.poetryfoundation.org/resources/learning/essays/detail/69384.
31 Vince, G. (2014). *Adventures in the Anthropocene: A journey to the heart of the planet we made.* Minneapolis, MN: Milkweed.
32 Ibid, p. 57.

Chapter 3

Encountering our world anew

Re-visioning nature

Earth isn't what it used to be. Let alone what we used to think it was. Our planet is changing rapidly. Lines are sky rocketing off climate scientists' graphs. Increasing levels of greenhouse gases, ocean acidification, species extinction, land and sea temperatures, are catapulting Earth into a geological age unlike any other known to humans.[1] Assumptions about Earth's infinite capacities and predictable ways, enshrined in modern societies, are not a good fit for today's ecologically disrupted world. Across the globe, people are having to re-vision Earth as increasing temperatures reveal the complex workings of our planet's dynamic biosphere. At the same time we are having to re-vision ourselves, as we wake up to the ecological impacts of how we live.

It can be tempting to project stories of human guilt and punishment onto the predicament of climate chaos. But simplistic narratives will not help us understand Earth's nature, nor our own, in these complex and fast-moving times. If we are to forge more informed and realistic views of our world and ourselves, we need to fantasise less about Earth, and focus more on the systemic nature of the biosphere and our place within this. Western philosophy has plentiful idealisations and denigrations of the natural world stretching back to the ancient Greeks. The present ecological crisis challenges us to lose such distorting fantasies about a world that is barely known, but heavily mythologised.

The very naming and framing of "Nature" is a mythic process which in the Western tradition suggests a separation between humans and world. For example, one story about Nature proposes that it is an innocent and peaceful Garden of Eden from which humans are exiled sinners. Another proposes that Nature is a dangerous and savage jungle, which humans must separate themselves from to become civilised. Each of these mythic projections assigns characteristics to the natural world founded upon moralistic judgements. Their agenda is driven by a process of human self-definition that determines "what is not me" or "what is not human." What is not identified as human, is disowned, and then projected onto Nature and judged as "other." As a result, Nature can be either idealised as perfect and harmonious, or demonised as hostile and harsh. This process of projection caters to a desire for certainty, understanding, judgement, control and separation at the cost of holding a larger view which tolerates openness, mystery, vulnerability and relatedness.

Sigmund Freud's view of nature both analysed and enshrined this projective view. He famously declared that "The principle task of civilisation, its actual raison d'être, is to defend us against nature." And that when "nature rises up against us, majestic, cruel and inexorable; she brings to our mind once more our weakness and helplessness, which we thought to escape through the work of civilisation."[2] His mythologising analysis portrays a defensive and victimised humanity within a persecutory natural world. It is a narrative that normalises separation and conflict between human and nature. It risks creating a self-fulfilling prophecy as societies that are hostile to natural processes are more likely to engender ecological destructions. While there may be some truth in Freud's observations, his framing and metaphors are deeply unhelpful for our times as they preclude human collaborations with the natural world.

New myths arise in times of extreme disruption, fuelled by understandings that illuminate unexpected circumstances and dispel habitual assumptions now proven false. A cascade of human-induced ecological disasters is stimulating new mythic views which recognise how all life forms on Earth, including human, are embedded in, and related to, one and other. They pay homage to Indigenous understandings while speaking the languages of biology, genetics, complexity and systems theories. Taken together, these views reveal the many ways that we are not separate from natural processes, but very much a part of them.

An ecological consciousness reshapes human identity and cultural views in ways that are both liberating and challenging. Timothy Morton, a philosopher who contests the very concept of nature declares:

I don't really believe in nature, I believe in ecology; I think nature is actually a human construct, I think that's what's wrong with it. It's not like I don't believe in coral, I do believe in coral which is why I don't believe in nature. And I think that not only is nature a human philosophical construct, an aesthetic construct, it's also a social construct that is one of the reasons for this [ecological] violence.[3]

Morton's rejection of nature as a human conception, based on the belief that something can be fully known and understood as one "thing" brings us closer to the mysteries, gaps and in-betweens of life. An ecological worldview takes away old blinkers, freeing the mind to uncertainty and a multiplicity of understandings that can illuminate Earth's processes, but never fully claim to know them. Replacing a fixed view of ourselves as a human species with an ecological one, helps us to focus primarily on the ways we interact with life and matter on Earth, rather than on our difference or separateness.

Evolving perspectives

Developing ecological awareness transforms consciousness. At a psychological level, this awareness unseats the ego, our habitual conscious sense of self, by bringing it into relationship with everything else on Earth, or indeed the cosmos. It's a dizzying shift to see a human being as a network of relationships, rather than as a solo traveller. For those of us who are accustomed to seeing ourselves through the individualistic myths of modern Western culture, it can feel like both a loss of autonomy and a gain in belonging.

Seeing ourselves as a part of our ecosystems, local and global, induces an Alice in Wonderland experience of feeling both smaller and bigger than our habitual selves. Australian author Tim Winton writes:

We're used to seeing ourselves as the pinnacle of reality. But travelling deep into landscape, paying attention to the natural world, we're reminded of our true position in the scheme of things. Yes, we are evolutionary inheritors of immense creativity and power, a fundamental terrestrial phenomenon ... yet we are, in the end, tiny.[4]

Experiencing our smallness in the universe induces existential anxiety. It also brings humility and perspective as the grip of ego is loosened. This is why so many spiritual retreats and quests take people into larger landscapes. The immensity of land, sea and sky helps to dissolve the ego's self-absorption.

Awareness of the climate crisis provokes something of the same experience. We can feel much smaller in a much larger canvas, triggering feelings of diminishment and disempowerment. We need to find ways of articulating and exploring such feelings with others. For those who have grown up in neoliberal societies, with their rhetoric about the virtues of individual autonomy and freedom, and their assumptions of human exceptionalism and endless growth, there is little recognition of the value or opportunities of accepting our smallness in relation to larger forces. Without this we lack not only perspective, but a solid ground of being in the world.

What we need to hear more about is how connecting our relative smallness to the vast networks of life expands consciousness and deepens identity. Smallness and largeness go hand in hand. In the words of mindfulness teacher and psychotherapist Richard Sears:

> The minerals in our blood and bones were literally created by the stars. We need air, water, earth, and other people just as much as we need our hearts, brains, and skin. By paying attention, we can more often notice and internalize the insight that our very existence is due to the contributions of countless other beings and processes. We are so much bigger than we realize.[5]

Acknowledging humanity's embeddedness in Earth's ecosystems cultivates an unconditional sense of belonging and connectedness. It is an inclusive stretch long held in many Indigenous cultures, but for those of us who have grown up within techno-industrial cultures it takes a significant stretch of the mind to open up to this deep experience of relatedness.

The proposed naming of the *Anthropocene* as our current geological epoch is one marker of changing consciousness about human–Earth relations, and the tensions that this can arouse. This naming, first formally proposed in 2000 by atmospheric chemist Paul Crutzen and aquatic biologist Eugene Stoermer,[6] acknowledges that contemporary human activity is leaving its markers in the geological record. It also proceeds from the recognition that the Holocene Epoch of the last 11,700 years, with its relatively steady climatic conditions, is over. Taking its place is an epoch of human-caused climate disruption, and species loss so massive that it is commonly referred to as the Sixth Great Extinction of Earth's history. The beginning of the Anthropocene is most commonly identified as 1945, following the release of atomic bombs, with the radioactive footprint providing evidence of human impact on the world's biosphere.

The naming of the Anthropocene, as a recognition of the interconnections between human activity and Earth's biosphere has caught the public imagination with its scientific underpinnings and mythic overtones. But there is also strong resistance to this naming, which has not yet been officially adopted by geological stratigraphers. Professor of Philosophy Christine J. Cuomo, argues against this naming on ethical grounds because of the risk of creating a grand narrative that signals an acceptance of the inevitability of human destructiveness and selfishness.[7] For her, this naming signals an acceptance of a new normal rather than an extreme crisis we must work to avoid.

The Anthropocene Alliance's response to Cuomo's argument was that far:

> from surrendering to catastrophe, scholars and activists who describe the current epoch with the label Anthropocene are sounding an alarm and calling for change at a local, national and global level. Humans now have the capacity to alter and indeed destroy the world.[8]

These two interpretations highlight psychological responses as much as philosophical and geological ones. For Cuomo the naming suggests surrender, while for Anthropocene advocates it works as an alarm. Both want action but have different instincts about what kind of narrative and symbolism might best achieve this.

There are other concerns aroused by the Anthropocene naming, many of them political. By emphasising human agency in general, the term glosses over the significant differences between the wealthy societies that drive climate disruption, and poorer societies who do not, but who are on the frontline of floods, drought and eroding coastlines. Some suggest *Capitalocene* would be a more accurate naming for our Epoch, as this names the economic system that is primarily responsible for driving up CO_2 levels, rather than tribal agriculture or hunter/gatherer societies. Another concerning aspect of the Anthropocene naming is the possibility that it might glorify human agency with worrying consequences. If, as the name suggests, humans, or to be strictly accurate "men," are the primary force in shaping Earth's eco-systems, perhaps they should go further by developing geo-engineering technologies to "manage" escalating greenhouse gas emissions. Should humans, in the words of futurist Stewart Brand become more godlike in our actions on Earth?[9] Or would we be better, as Paul Kingsnorth suggests, to '"unhumanize" our views' by relinquishing "the notion that only humans matter, or that humans are in control, even of themselves"?[10] I find these debates rich with possibilities for provoking people into deeper questions about identity, agency and humankind's place on Earth. They are a crucial part of working through our situation. Because of them, many issues – spiritual, philosophical, political, practical – are being brought into consciousness in a new way, along with an increased sensitivity to the importance of symbolism and narrative. This is an important part of the process of the disintegration of old myths about the world and the evolution of new ones.

The most transformative debates move beyond old binaries which insist on an *either/or* perspective. Whenever we are caught in a binary of oppositions, our minds become handicapped by what we do not want to see or acknowledge. However, if both positions can be consciously maintained and explored, in what Carl Jung described as a "holding of the tension of opposites," it facilitates the transcending of one-sided positions. Jung wrote:

> The confrontation of ... [opposing] positions generates a tension charged with energy and creates a living, third thing – not a logical stillbirth ... but a movement out of the suspension between opposites, a living birth that leads to a new level of being, a new situation.[11]

With this consciousness shift, new creative possibilities can emerge that are able to acknowledge the "truths" of both positions, and then go beyond them. Holding the tension of the opposites in relation to the Anthropocene naming means accepting that the human species has the capacity to be both powerful and powerless in our relationship to the biosphere, and then finding a way to creatively proceed within this understanding.

The responses needed to address the climate crisis have to be innovative, given that humanity is facing an entirely new problem of its own making. There will inevitably be trials and errors of wide-ranging proportions. But single-minded approaches of any sort cannot be feasible, as they lack systemic attention. Climate initiatives need to draw on ecological, technological, ethical, sociological, psychological and political understandings as well as huge dollops of creative imagination. So many debates provoked by climate disruption are oppositional and binary in their thinking, both within ourselves, and between one and other. This too is the struggle between old and new myths at work. It is painful to participate in and to observe, as it expresses a refusal to sit with the opposing conflicts and birth of a new worldview. Nevertheless, at times, the repeated articulation and consideration of oppositional positions does precede the emergence of a third way. If we can recognise how one-sided positions warp perceptions by oppressing aspects of ourselves, others and our world, it allows us to move beyond divisive and scapegoating thinking. Transcending the deadlock of oppositional thinking, we can proceed from *either/or* to *both/and*. This shift matures consciousness as it crafts more comprehensive and less divisive understandings.

Grieving the losses

As engagement with the climate crisis broadens ecological consciousness, it presses hard upon the heart. The more we love, the more we feel the loss of what we love. Climate disruption losses can be visceral for those who feel strongly connected to a place or ecosystem. Journalist and mountaineer Dahr Jamail writes:

> ... every time I learn of the collapse of yet another massive glacial system, or the baring of a magnificent peak that was once gleaming in ice and snow, it feels like a punch in my stomach. Like I've lost a close relative, or a good friend. Again.[12]

There is so much to mourn on Earth right now: the extinction of species, the death of coral reefs, the melting of glaciers and the battering of communities from intense cyclones, bush fires, droughts and floods. The biologist E.O. Wilson suggests that our current age be called the *Age of Eremocene* or Age of Loneliness, marking the extremity of ongoing species losses.[13] Grief runs deep through the veins of many. Climate psychologist Per Espen Stoknes calls this "the Great Grief, a feeling rising in us as if from the earth itself at this time."[14] Yet this deep sorrow is rarely expressed in public discussions about the climate crisis. Too often grief goes unnamed and unhonoured, although it is inseparable from our lives in this age of ecological destructions.

Psychological theories across the field agree on the importance of grieving our losses, from the highly personal through to the broadly collective. Grief is a dynamic emotional process integral to consciousness. At a psychological level, it supports us to both face into our own and others' vulnerability, transience and mortality, and to repair life energy after significant loss. Grief work honours the loss, the sadness and the experience of diminishment or absence, while also tilling the ground for self-transformation and the continuation of life. Psychotherapist Fran Weller describes grief work is "an act of devotion, rooted in love and compassion" that requires "an ongoing practice of deepening, attending and listening."[15] When we grieve for what is lost, it clears the way towards a strengthening of love and commitment for what remains. In time this may build a desire to make good from the loss by repairing what damages we can and/or compensating for them. Grief can make us both very sad and very motivated to act.

Many traditional cultures have rituals of mourning that give full weight and time to the psychological work of grieving. Wailing, laments, poems, storytelling and periods of retreat all play a part in expressing and ritualising loss in the company of others. However, most people in contemporary cultures have lost these traditional mourning rituals and with them the ability to grieve well. Grief has become a taboo emotion which can leave those who are mourning feeling isolated, without sufficient acknowledgement, support or containers for the intense and raw emotions they are experiencing. To grieve well we need to be able to share our sorrows and feel some sense of belonging with others. When we experience this, we can in turn hold and comfort others in their grief.

Western psychological theories of grief often focus on bereavement; however, grief surfaces across the whole spectrum of our life and selves. It can take many forms, including loss of identity, innocence, aspiration, belonging, self-esteem as well as home, relationship, place and ultimately life itself. Sometimes we find ways to recognise and honour this, with the support of others, at other times grief goes unnamed and can become subsumed into a generalised feeling of depression. When grief is not named and attended to, it "condemns us to a life shadowed by grief" writes Weller.[16] The losses live on, but being unhonoured, they tend to separate us from life, rather than weave us into feelings of belonging within the fabric of life's dark and light spaces.

Grief haunts communities as well as individuals. Over thirty years ago, Jungian analyst James Hillman spoke eloquently about the psychological cost of living in destructive societies, suggesting that:

> The depression we're all trying to avoid could very well be a prolonged reaction to what we've been doing to the world, a mourning and grieving for what we're doing to nature and to cities and to whole peoples – the destruction of a lot of our world. We may be depressed partly because this is the soul's reaction to the mourning and grieving that we're not consciously doing.[17]

Since Hillman wrote this, climate disruption has intensified grief over what we are doing to our world. Very slowly, this is beginning to be acknowledged and named as ecological worldviews find more traction.

Renee Lertzman believes that "environmental melancholia" is widespread in modern communities as a result of unrecognised ecological losses and arrested mourning. In order to support engagement with environmental issues she writes "we need to understand how losses have been sustained, worked with psychically and socially, experienced, survived and mourned."[18] Where there is no naming of loss and working through of grief, people's feelings remain unconscious, conflicted and confused, sapping energy and direction for ecological care and repair. Encouragingly, Lertzman identifies surprisingly mundane remedies, such as publishing editorials in newspapers and "designing messaging and framing that acknowledges loss while pointing to what is taking place to repair and restore" as effective ways to boost community response.[19] Grieving is an innate human healing process. We do not need to design complex ways to do it. But we do need to recognise the ways that we, individually and collectively, suppress grief by not acknowledging loss, nor the sadness, guilt and other feelings that accompany this.

In the research group I facilitated it took some time for us to be able to acknowledge and speak openly of the grief most of us felt in response to climate disruption. When we did have in-depth discussions about grief and mourning, one thread of the conversation was about how some people resisted these feelings because they represented a form of surrender. As one person said, "Grief seems to be like there's no hope, if there's grief you've lost ... It seems like if I felt grief, then I wouldn't feel like doing anything about it." This is not an uncommon attitude, especially amongst activists and campaigners, where grieving can be seen as a giving up. Beneath this attitude can be a deeper anxiety that, once grief is allowed to surface, there will be no end to it, sapping energy for action. This is not an unreasonable fear, given that climate and ecological losses are accelerating with no foreseeable end in sight.

However, research into climate grief suggests there can be a trajectory of healing and psychological development for those who do consciously acknowledge and express their grief, especially when they are well-supported by peers, counsellors, groups or communities.[20] This was the case in my research group where each person could take time to explore what climate grief meant and felt like for themselves. The discussion that started out with fears that grieving would lessen hope and action, ended with an acknowledgement that grief and hope were not mutually exclusive emotions. The group also recognised that being able to mourn together helped each of us to engage with present ecological losses and the lack of certainty ahead. One of the reasons that our conversations were able to move on from apocalyptic imaginings, I believe, was because we became more able to name and feel grief over climate losses happening in the present. This brought our conversations into a more grounded reality where our future imaginings could be more curious and less fearful, opening up a range of paths for possible action.

Joanna Macy has plenty of experience of living with ongoing grief over the losses of the world while sustaining active hope for addressing this. Weaving together insights from systems theory, Buddhism, environmental science and eco-philosophy, Macy has done pioneering work supporting personal and social change. Her project called *The Work That Reconnects*, encourages people to be fully present to the destructions of contemporary life, which she says is "The most radical thing any of us can do at this time."[21] To do this she believes people need to come together to face into grief and despair, in order to be able to deepen compassion and the motivation to act. This, she says, is the way "to come home to a larger identity and belonging."

Joanna Macy's approach worked for Dahl Jamail, who became depressed and traumatised following his work as a reporter on the frontlines of the Iraq war. After attending one of Macy's workshops he wrote that becoming fully present to the world broke his heart but "then I saw how despair transforms, in the face of overwhelming social and ecological crises, into clarity of vision, then into constructive, collaborative action."[22] Macy emphasises how vital it is that this transformative work be done with others. In her own experience:

> Just hearing the news of what is happening each day on the planet, I can't handle all of it alone. I'm not supposed to. Even looking at it requires we reach out to each other and take each other's arm and I can tell you how I feel, and you will listen. The very steps we need to take bring us the relief and reward of the whole point of it, which is our collective nature, our non-separateness, because this is the only thing that can save us.[23]

Sharing grief affirms communal life. It fuels conversations about what matters most, making fertile ground for initiatives based on common values.

The Dark Mountain Project is one initiative which has grown out of shared grief for the ecological destructions of this age. Founded in 2009 by Paul Kingsnorth and Doug Hines, it started out as an online "network of writers, artists and thinkers who have stopped believing the stories our civilisation tells itself."[24] On later reflection, Kingsnorth recognises that Dark Mountain also provides:

> ... a way to work through the grief caused by the end of much of what we hold dear ... Before you can move on, before you can accept what has happened and come to terms with it, you need to be able to grieve, in the company of others.[25]

Over time, the Dark Mountain Project has evolved into a creative enterprise that has organised festivals, published anthologies and spawned international groups. The shared grieving has laid foundations and released energy for cultural projects "rooted in place, time and nature" which imaginatively engage with what lies ahead as well as what is behind.

Grief is neither one-dimensioned nor one-storied. It mourns what is lost and marks the pain of absence while preparing the ground for new life. Well-honoured grief transforms, inspiring compassion, connection and creative responses. Joining with others through conversations, writing, rituals or memorials to bear witness to climate upheaval, species extinctions and other ecological destructions is crucial psychological work for the world right now. Without this we cannot face into the losses of our era, nor birth the energy and heart for transforming how we understand ourselves and live in a conscious relationship to our planet.

Meeting mortality

Life and death go hand in hand. But they are not equally welcomed. We humans, with all our abilities for forward thinking, have developed a severe death anxiety. This anxiety has fuelled many attempts to sail beyond the horizons of mortality. All for nought, so far. But death anxiety ensures that we keep trying, both literally and symbolically. And in doing so we fight the natural processes and limits of existence.

In his classic book *The Denial of Death*, anthropologist Ernest Becker argued that people struggle against death by embarking on "immortality projects" grounded in heroic worldviews.[26] What this means is that people believe and do what they can to establish a feeling of having enduring significance in the larger universe, in order to navigate death anxieties. This, writes Becker, is the human response to the existential dilemma of having both a mortal animal body and a symbolic sense of self which strives for eternal life.

Subsequent research based on Becker's arguments, known as Terror Management Theory, repeatedly demonstrates that when people are confronted with thoughts of death, the defence of their worldviews strengthens. This theory gives one explanation of why, when people hear about climate disruption with all of its reminders of loss, death and extinctions, deniers become more denialist, while believers become more fervent in their beliefs, setting the stage for intense polarised debates. Another unconscious response to climate disruption that Terror Management Theory sheds light on is the increased urge to cling to self-esteem and status-boosting "immortality projects" when given reminders of death. In contemporary societies, this typically takes the form of consumerism. Buying endless amounts of stuff, building grand homes, travelling to exotic destinations and driving SUVs can all be unconscious responses to death anxiety. Anthropologist Janis Dickinson describes this conundrum as the "people paradox," where "the very things that bring us symbolic immortality often conflict with our prospects for survival."[27] Consequently, the more the general populace hears about climate crisis and its deathly associations, the more that they may unconsciously attempt to cement the solidity of their lives, very often in ways that are ecologically damaging.

When death denying behaviours in a society become overwhelmingly self-destructive, a counterbalancing pressure to consciously face into death arises. Research shows that defences against death anxiety lessen with conscious contemplation and rational awareness of death.[28] Consciously reflecting upon death has become a contemporary phenomenon as the sway of traditional religions, with their set beliefs about death and the afterlife, loses hold. Death cafes and salons are mushrooming around the world, while books about mortality, such as Atul Gawande's *Being Mortal* and Paul Kalanithi's *When Breath Becomes Air*, are on bestseller lists. It seems the circumstances of the times is demanding collective reflection upon death, in order to incubate a more conscious response to it.

The climate crisis can be a major stimulus for increasing consciousness about death. In my research group, death proved to be a high-ranking topic, without any particular prompting from me. Personal encounters with death, experiences of being with the dying, hopes and fears about our own deaths and beliefs about the afterlife or lack of it were all spontaneously shared. While this may sound gloomy, it was actually very freeing and life affirming. A number of us commented that they felt less fearful of death and more resilient as a result of our ruminations upon our own and others' mortality.

While every person carries their own individual experiences, meanings and feelings around death, at a collective level climate disruption is stimulating eco-systemic views of life and death. These views affirm the necessity of death in order to further life and evolutionary processes. They provide some scope for symbolic immortality through an identification with Earth, or the energetic nature of life. For writer Diane Ackerman, understanding herself as nature brings comfort in life and death:

> All of our being, juices, flesh and spirit occurs as nature; nature surrounds, permeates, effervesces in, and includes us. At the end of our days it deranges and dissembles us like old toys banished to the basement. There, once living beings, we return to our non-living elements, but still and forever remain a part of nature.[29]

As well as finding symbolic immortality through a sense of everlasting belonging within Earth's fabric, there is also the possibility of consciously taking on the preservation of our planet and its ecosystems as a kind of cultural "immortality project" which satisfies existential desires for symbolic perpetuation and meaning in life. Conservation projects help to bridge seemingly opposing worldviews. Janis Dickinson observes:

Love of nature is a deep ethical and spiritual issue that is consistent with most belief systems. Preservation of land, species conservation, and the creation of innovative technologies to combat the problem of climate change provide profound opportunities for symbolic immortality.[30]

One immortality project that is rapidly increasing in response to the climate crisis is tree planting. Land clearing across the world is a major contributor to rising greenhouse emissions. It also causes serious soil erosion. Saving forests, planting trees and restoring carbon rich soils are crucial legacies we can gift our planet right now.

In 1977, a tree planting project, known as the Green Belt Movement, was founded by Wangari Maathai in Kenya in response to creeping desertification. This initiative has planted well over forty million trees, reclaimed and restored forest lands as well as advocated for human rights and democracy. Maathai understood tree planting as both an ecological and spiritual practice which brought her close to the act of creation and to the elements.[31] It also made her feel "part and parcel of that earth," in life or after death. For Maathai, the experience of living on beyond death through tree planting fitted in with the beliefs of her ancestral peoples, the Kikuyu, who feel the ground, forests and mountains are where their relatives are, both those yet to be born and those who died. This is a form of symbolic immortality that encourages care for the Earth because as Maathai says "You couldn't destroy the land because you were destroying your ancestors, and if you did you'd have nowhere to go when you died or no place to be born into."[32]

But you don't have to been born into an Indigenous culture to resonate with such Earth-centred views. Another revered woman who plants trees is British actress Dame Judi Dench who has created a wood in remembrance of friends, relatives and actors who have died. Dench names the trees she plants after dead loved ones, regarding them as her extended family who become more wonderful as time goes on.[33] Giving symbolic immortality to her loved ones in this way, has engendered a passion for trees in Dench. After studying with Tony Kirkham, Head of the Arboretum at Royal Botanical Gardens Kew for a year, Dench developed an ecological appreciation for the way that trees in forests communicate and share with each other through their root systems and other forms of signalling. She reflects that when she planted memorial trees for her friends she had hoped that they would form a community, and now she has learnt that this is in fact true.[34] An eco-systemic understanding of our world fosters a sense of eternity through its life/death/life cycles. When we understand that human beings are a part of this, we can find immortality in mortality, by meeting death on biological and symbolic grounds in ways that nurture love for our Earth and deep comfort for ourselves.

Loving Earth well

Cherishing Earth's beauty is perhaps the greatest healing we can bring to our world and ourselves. There is so much to marvel about as we learn more about the intricacies and elegance of our world's ecosystems, and so much to love; both with an instinctive awe that has long been a part of the human psyche, and with a conscious appreciation informed by the latest research. Climate crisis in particular is stirring humanity into a fresh view of our Earth along with a new imagining of our place within it. Psychoanalyst Sally Weintrobe writes that this new imagining "enables us to love the Earth more fully and in a more mature way," which includes being able to consciously acknowledge "our true dependency on and indebtedness to the Earth."[35] This new imagining enlivens what has often been blank space for people who have been disconnected from the ground from which their being grows.

One of the ways that we are seeing a rise of a more conscious love for our world is through the increasing popularity of nature writing, especially writing that responds to the dilemmas of the Anthropocene era. This "new nature writing" explores human–nature relatedness, bearing in mind the tensions, tears and terrors of climate change and mass extinctions. Australian author James Bradley describes this writing as being "animated by a profound ethical urgency, an understanding that in the twenty-first century to write about nature is a political act, a way of bearing witness to the ecocide humans are inflicting on the biosphere."[36] Writers such as George Monbiot, Paul Kingsnorth, Diane Ackerman, Terry Tempest Williams, Robert MacFarlane and many others face into ecological destructions, analysing the causes, while maintaining a delight and awe in the beauties and terrors of the world. They open doors to an informed, present and deeply appreciative way of being consciously connected to Earth which can bear witness to the destructions, the healings and the ongoing revelations of ecosystems.

Grief, joy, scientific research, social analysis and personal reflection all have their place in an encounter with today's climate-disrupted world. There is so much to get one's head and heart around as the British poet Melanie Challoner found out when she wrote her book, *On Extinction*, in order to understand more about her own and others' estrangement from the natural world. Studying places of extinction over several years changed Challoner. She developed a sense of her own place in the land, along with a deep love for flora and fauna. This brought her a joy which she understood was all the more acute because it was grounded in awareness of loss, including the loss of inherited knowledge about land and places. She wrote:

> While my pleasure proceeded from an intrinsic desire to discover and understand my landscape, I knew why it was a joy, and knew – more significantly – why it *had* to be joy. Although the beauty of the wild flowers may have made me notice them, it was my sense of their imperilment, that inspired my knowledge of them, and the more I knew of both the wild flowers and the animals around them, the more I was motivated in my occupation. … My observation of wild flowers and the pleasure I took in them was intimately bound to a conscious and moral reclamation of knowledge.[37]

Developing knowledge about, and relationship with, the natural world through education, connection and observation transforms us and the world. Joy, grief, curiosity, tenderness and awe are easily stirred when we bring full attention to Earth's ways and her current plights. Hope can feature too. Bradley writes that if "there's beauty as well as grief, then we are reminded that not everything is lost."[38] Making ourselves open and vulnerable to this most primal connection while informing ourselves about what we are observing in today's world works the ground for new myths and imaginings. Ones that change visions, stir minds and hearts, transform values and motivate actions.

There is no definitive map for how to engage with Earth's beauty and marvels, but there are plenty of invitations. For me, living close to Sydney's CBD, a daily invitation arrives with the shifting sounds and rhythms of the dawn chorus. The calls of currawongs, kookaburras, lorikeets and Indian mynahs swoop through the roars of a nearby motorway and landing planes. Sometimes it's all I hear, other times I have to choose to listen. I pay heed to Diane Ackerman's advice that "We can't enchant the world, which makes its own magic; but we can enchant ourselves by paying deep attention."[39] Ackerman has spent a life time paying deep attention to the wonders, complexities and fragilities of the world. She observes:

> The freedom of unbridling the self and losing it in nature is immeasurable. Alive moments can be anytime anywhere. If I closely watch any natural wonder, really watch it, non-judgementally, in the present moment, noting its nuances, how it looks in changing light, or on different days, yet remains recognizably the same, then the world becomes dearer and less trying, and priorities rearrange themselves with an almost audible clicking.[40]

Consciously engaging with where we live – in place and in body – retrains attention in rewarding ways. The busy-ness of modern life with all of its abstractions and distractions gives way to the body's natural processes of sensing and breathing. Dropping the agendas that so often distance ourselves from what sustains life brings to consciousness the ways we are *in* and *of* this world. The beauties, wounds, griefs, mysteries, terrors, and complexities of the world are all part of us. The more we can accept this, the more we can appreciate, understand, and collaborate with the natural processes of our planet.

Psychotherapist and pilgrimage leader Veronica Goodchild speaks about how walking in France in a state of gentle awareness became a form of teaching for her about how to relate to the natural world. She remembers:

> Walking became a kind of dreaming while awake. And my experience was that … I was being taught that despite the horrors of climate change (and the results of oceans heating up, and the ice melting, and species extinction, and all of that), I was being taught not to sink with the ship or fall into a kind of depression *only* about it. I was taught that there are ways that I could, just in my own small way, connect with nature by noticing her and noticing the different denizens of nature – the rocks, the bees, trees, and atmospheres in forests – and then, afterwards, as you do with a dream, I would keep a record of my experiences in a journal. Then I would deepen my experiences through research and ongoing exploration, so that it wasn't just a one-off thing, but it unfolded into quite an extraordinary journey.[41]

Approaching our world with attention dissolves the disconnections and distractions that underlie climate inaction. It also nurtures a love for the world which is joyous and motivating.

When interviewed about his lifelong vocation, marine scientist Charlie Veron, a world authority on coral, said "I started working on corals because I fell in love with them ... It became, really, a part of me."[42] Loving the world, or any part of it, becomes a part of who we are. We and every other organism on this planet, are relational beings formed by, and ever in motion within, the dance of Earth's matter. This biologically based paradigm of consciousness transforms identity and changes values. Not only does it demolish myths about human identity being separated from the world, it also acts as a catalyst for maturing processes.

Ecological consciousness challenges and dismantles self-centred feelings of entitlement. We start to grow up. And this changes everything, how we see the world, who we think we are, what we do and where we belong. The recognition of our embeddedness within the world gifts a sense of belonging, relatedness and worth which lives far beyond the isolations and constraints of self-centredness. Arriving at the understanding that we are not *apart from* but an active *part of* the most beautiful world we can ever know, expands horizons, changes perspectives, transforms identity, opens hearts and develops relatedness, as we explore further in the next chapter.

Notes

1 Steffen, W., Grinevald, J., Crutzen, P. & McNeill, J. (2011, Jan 31). The Anthropocene: Conceptual and historical perspectives. *Philosophical Transactions of the Royal Society A*. Retrieved from https://royalsociety publishing.org/doi/full/10.1098/rsta.2010.0327
2 Freud. S. (1962). *The future of an illusion*. London, UK: The Hogarth Press, pp.11–12.
3 Morton, T. (2014). Timothy Morton & Hans Ulrich Obrist: A conversation held on the occasion of the Serpentine Galleries Extinction Marathon: Visions of the Future. *Dis Magazine*. Retrieved from http://dismagazine.com/disillusioned/discussion-disillusioned/68280/hans-ulrich-obrist-timothy-morton/
4 Winton, T. (2015). *Island home: A landscape memoir*. London, UK: Hamish Hamilton, p. 225.
5 Sears, R. W. (2014). *Mindfulness: Living through challenges and enriching your life in this moment*. Chichester, UK: Wiley, p. 13.
6 MacFarlane, R. (2016). Generation Anthropocene; How humans have altered the planet forever. *The Guardian*. Retrieved from www.theguardian.com/books/2016/apr/01/generation-anthropocene-altered-planet-for-ever

7   Christine J. Cuomo. (2017, Sep 20). Comment: The Anthropocene: Foregone or premature conclusion? Examining the ethical implications of naming a new epoch. *Earth*. Retrieved from www.earthmagazine.org/art icle/comment-anthropocene-foregone-or-premature-conclusion-examining-ethical-implications-naming

8   Taking on a critic of the Anthropocene concept. (2017, Nov 28). Retrieved from https://anthropocenealliance.org/blog/2017/11/28/taking-on-a-critic-of-the-anthropocene-concept

9   Brand, S. (1968, Sep). We are as gods. *The Whole Earth Catalog*. Retrieved from www.wholeearth.com/issue/1010/article/195/we.are.as.gods

10 Kingsnorth, P. (2017). *Confessions of a recovering environmentalist*. London, UK: Faber & Faber, p. 230.

11 Jung, C. G. (1969). *The structure and dynamics of the psyche* (2nd ed. CW Vol. 8). London, UK: Routledge & Kegan Paul, p. 90.

12 Jamail, D. (2014, Jun 3). On staying sane in a suicidal culture. *Truthout*. Retrieved from www.truth-out.org/news/item/24083-on-staying-sane-in-a-suicidal-culture

13 Wilson, E. O. (2013, Nov 18). Beware the age of loneliness. *The Economist*. Retrieved from www.economist.com/news/21589083-man-must-do-more-preserve-rest-life-earth-warns-edward-o-wilson-professor-emeritus.

14 Stoknes, P. E. (2015). *What we think about when we try not to think about global warming*. White River Junction, VT: Chelsea Green, p. 171.

15 Weller, F. (2015). *The wild edge of sorrow: Rituals of renewal and the sacred work of grief*. Berkeley, CA: North Atlantic Books, p. 5.

16 Ibid, p. 9.

17 Hillman, J. & Ventura, M. (1992). *We've had a hundred years of psychotherapy and the world's getting worse*. New York, NY: HarperCollins, p. 45.

18 Lertzman, R. A. (2015). *Environmental melancholia: Psychoanalytic dimensions of engagement*. Hove, UK: Routledge, p. 101.

19 Ibid.

20 Hoggett, P. & Randall, R. Outriders of the coming adversity: How climate activists and climate scientists keep going. Retrieved from www.climatepsychologyalliance.org/explorations/blogs/173-outriders-of-the-coming-adversity-how-climate-activists-and-climate-scientists-keep-going

21 Jamail, D. (2014, Jun 3). On staying sane in a suicidal culture. *Truthout*. Retrieved from www.truth-out.org/news/item/24083-on-staying-sane-in-a-suicidal-culture

22 Ibid.

23 Ibid.

24 Dark Mountain Project. (2013, Jan 2). Dark mountain 3. *Resilience*. Retrieved from www.resilience.org/resources/dark-mountain-3/

25 Kingsnorth, P. (2017). *Confessions of a recovering environmentalist*. London, UK: Faber & Faber, p. 98.

26 Becker, E. (1973). *The denial of death*. New York, NY: Free Press.

27 Dickinson, J. L. (2009). The people paradox: Self-esteem striving, immortality ideologies, and human response to climate change. *Ecology and Society*, 14 (1). www.ecologyandsociety.org/vol14/iss1/art34/

28 Ibid.

29 Ackerman, D. (2009). Dawn light: Dancing with cranes and other ways to start the day. New York, NY: WW Norton, p. 3.
30 Dickinson, J. L. (2009). The people paradox: Self-esteem striving, immortality ideologies, and human response to climate change. *Ecology and Society*, 14 (1). www.ecologyandsociety.org/vol14/iss1/art34/
31 Parabola Editors. (2017, Jan 24). The tree of life: An interview with Wangari Maathai. Parabola. Retrieved from https://parabola.org/2017/01/24/the-tree-of-life-an-interview-with-wangari-maathai/
32 Ibid.
33 Knapton, S. (2017, Dec 7). Dame Judi Dench: My life now is just trees and champagne. *The Telegraph*. Retrieved from www.telegraph.co.uk/science/2017/12/07/dame-judi-dench-life-now-just-trees-trees-champagne/
34 Ibid.
35 Weintrobe, S. (2015, Dec 2). A new imagination. Retrieved from www.climatepsychologyalliance.org/explorations/papers/103-anew-imagination
36 Bradley, J. (2017, Feb 21). Writing on the precipice. Sydney Review of Books. Retrieved from http://sydneyreviewofbooks.com/writing-on-the-precipice-climate-change/
37 Challoner, M. (2012). *On extinction: How we became estranged from nature*. Berkeley, CA: Counterpoint, p. 298.
38 Brady, A. (2017, Oct 30). How will climate change affect your grandchildren? Chicago Review of Books. Retrieved from https://chireviewofbooks.com/2017/10/24/burning-worlds-james-bradley-clade-interview/
39 Ackerman, D. (2009). Dawn light: Dancing with cranes and other ways to start the day. New York, NY: WW Norton, p. 237.
40 Ibid, p. 54.
41 Goodchild, V. (2019). Dreams, synchronicities and our relationship to the Earth. In B. Bright & J. P. Marshall (Eds.), *Earth, climate dreams: Dialogues with depth psychologists in the age of the Anthropocene*. Honolulu, HI: Depth Insights, pp. 301–332.
42 Miller, G. (2016, Oct 31). Climate scientists feel weight of world on their shoulders. *Earshot*. Retrieved from www.abc.net.au/news/2016-10-31/climate-scientists-feel-weight-of-world-on-their-shoulders/7972452

Chapter 4

Extending horizons

Shifting identity

In contemporary cultures, where traditional religious perspectives are fading, defining yourself and your life's purpose can be a major pursuit and preoccupation. Contemporary economists, politicians, psychologists, sociologists, philosophers and New Age gurus offer a diverse array of answers to the existential questions of human being. Most of their offerings come with assumptions about *human exceptionalism*, the belief that human individuals are special, different and separate from the Earth, and all her other beings. *Exceptionalist views* of ourselves exile us from a sense of belonging in our world, or a sense of purpose grounded in being part of life on Earth. Identity becomes unmoored from life itself.

The deep ecology movement proceeds from the fundamental insight that underlying all contemporary environmental problems is the illusion of separation between human beings and the natural world.[1] Now, this insight is entering into mainstream thought. The climate crisis in particular is acting as a catalyst for questioning exceptionalist views of ourselves and our lives. Perceiving how our lives are woven into the fabric of Earth opens up existential discussions about who we are, what matters most and what gives us life. When we relinquish narrow and conditioned understandings of ourselves based upon exceptionalist assumptions, it reveals a world of connections and wonder. Biologist David George Haskell writes "Knowledge is relationship, belonging is spiritual knowledge."[2] Human life becomes a lot less lonely and a lot more sacred when it is understood as an interactive dance within a network of other life forms. Community and care for ongoing life become essential values, recasting personal desires and meaning within the context of being a participant in the web of life.

Changing consciousness wakes us up not only to our world and its complexities, but to the complexity of ourselves. There is a lot more in all of us than one identity, one viewpoint or one life. Just as the climate crisis alerts us to what has been ignored, forgotten and marginalised in the world, it can also wake us up to forms of knowing that have been buried within ourselves, such as nature relatedness, body awareness, intuitive knowings and spiritual connections. Beyond our conscious intelligence or sensibility, dreams researcher Susannah Benson notes there is an unconscious intelligence in each of us which keeps us alive. "We may not understand it, but it's vital to us, and seems part of what has to be recognised when listening to nature."[3] Bringing attention to what we habitually ignore or repress in ourselves challenges the power of the ego, or conscious sense of self. It allows us to recognise the unconscious disconnections or *splits* that exist within ourselves, as well as between us, others and the world. This is an unsettling and illuminating process, but if we can stay open to it, there are opportunities for psychological self-transformation along with re-visioned views of our life and world.

The development of an ecological sense of self is the basis for in-depth engagement with, and creative responses to, ecological crises. Deep ecologist John Seed writes:

> ecological ideas are not enough, we need an ecological identity, an ecological self. Ideas only engage one part of our brain, the frontal lobe, cognition. We need ecological feelings and actions as well as ideas to nurture ecological identity.[4]

Nurturing an ecological identity is a deep psychological process that requires reflection, time and companionship, as well as a willingness to undergo periods of confusion and emotional upheaval. Identifying and feeling the symptoms of loss, sickness, instability and imbalance within ourselves, as well as in the world, are all a part of this process. Ecopsychologist Mary-Jayne Rust describes the processes of "embodiment and recovering an intimacy with the other than human world" as both joyful and painful, involving "all the fears, hurts, losses, grief and trauma, that may accompany love in any reciprocal relationship."[5] Greater ecological connection heightens feelings of vulnerability, compassion and appreciation, potentially healing feelings of isolation and emptiness which are endemic in contemporary cultures.

The Natural Change Project provides us with stories about what ecologically inspired personal and social change looks and feels like. This project was pioneered in Scotland under the auspices of the World Wildlife Fund, "to catalyse and support personal, cultural and structural change that will lead to greater ecological sustainability."[6] Grounded in ecopsychological principles, the Natural Change Project worked to align psychological experience with biological reality, helping people to find their identity within the interconnections of the natural world. Its six-month programmes were created for people in leadership with the aim of encouraging the development of an ecological self as the foundation for personal change, social action and leadership initiatives. Activities ranged from co-counselling, guided meditations, storytelling, artmaking, solo retreats in both wilderness and urban areas, undertaking research into social change movements and exploring identity and consumerism. Participants shared stories about their experiences on the Natural Change website, providing insights into the psychological process of ecologically inspired consciousness change. Their many accounts of slowing down, heightening sensory awareness, appreciating the natural world, accepting emotional ups and downs, questioning values, strengthening intuitions, exploring feelings of interconnectedness and clarifying directions highlight common experiences in the development of an ecological sense of self.

The Natural Change Project also increased motivation and commitment to protect and care for the web of life. Reflecting on her experience in this programme, L. Macdonald wrote:

So ... has it worked then?
The simple, "surface" answer is yes ... it's made me think more about the whole range of interconnected themes around nature and our relationship with it ... it's made me act different – from changing my shopping habits, to introducing new sustainable procurement policies at work to feeding the birds ...
The more complex answer is ... it has worked, but
... in ways it is so hard to articulate, because the impact has affected me inside and out, at every level.
... in ways that have made my life much harder, not easier–deep questioning of your values in relation to the world will do that ...

... in ways that have led to huge frustration – particularly around the issues of engaging the public in tackling environmental issues....

... in ways that have led me to uncomfortable truths around choices I have made in the past, but equally having given me the tools to be kind to myself, to understand and forgive, and appreciate what it really is to be human.[7]

The effects of ecologically based consciousness change are deep and wide ranging. It is not just a change of thinking and behaviours but a reworking of identity and emotional patterning. Natural Change participants typically reported feeling more alive and hyper-aware of the beauty of the world, other people and the lessons of life, as well as more humble and compassionate. Life becomes more challenging, enlivening and purposeful as an embodied awareness of ecological crisis and complexity sharpens.

While the Natural Change Project is no longer running in Scotland, its work role models how individuals and groups can foster the development of an ecological self. In particular it highlights the key elements for deepening and embedding ecological awareness within self-identity:

- *Communion with the natural world*
- *Reflective and creative processes*
- *Community conversations*
- *Peer support and mentorship.*

Engaging with climate crisis can be a catalyst for embarking on this psychological process if it intensifies focus on our natural world and our place within it and spurs reflective conversations in the company of supportive others. For this to happen, engagement needs to extend beyond understanding the graphs and critiquing the politics into an embodied experience of Earth connectedness that protects and cares for the web of life as our own.

Enlivening connections

When our world is harmed, so too are we as a part of Earth's being. Human driven climate disruption is both ecological destruction and self-harm. Making the connection between the health of our ecosystems and the health of ourselves, starting with our bodies, lays foundations for holistic healing approaches that work from global ecosystems through to personal ones. In many ways, developing an ecological sense of self restores and re-stories individuals and cultures.

Naomi Klein has written in a very personal way about making the connection between Earth's body and her body, when she experienced miscarriages and conception difficulties in the midst of her climate campaign work. While she tried to keep her public life dealing with ecological crisis separate from her personal struggles, Klein eventually came to the realisation that "What I was learning about the ecological crisis informed the responses to my own fertility crisis; and what I learned about fertility began to leave its mark on how I saw the ecological crisis."[8] Making the connection between the struggles of her own body and the body of Earth was both distressing and illuminating for Klein as she recognised how her own fertility issues mirrored a growing trend of fertility disruptions in human communities and in other species as a result of climate disruption and polluting petro-chemical industries.

This feeling of commonality struck her most acutely when she was taken into the Mississippi River Delta following the Louisiana BP oil spill. Here she learnt about the decimation of fish spawn by oil slicks and gained new perspective on her own fertility problems:

> As our boat rocked in that terrible place ... I had the distinct feeling that we were suspended not in water but in amniotic fluid, immersed in a massive multi-species miscarriage ....
>
> It was then that I let go of the idea that infertility made me some sort of exile from nature, and began to feel what I can only describe as a kinship of the infertile. It suddenly dawned on me that I was indeed part of a vast biotic community, and it was a place where a great many of us – humans and nonhuman alike – found ourselves engaged in an uphill battle to create living beings.[9]

Identifying the commonality of her loss and grief with others lessened Klein's feelings of isolation. It also prompted her to think about the central importance of valuing and protecting the reproductive processes and the fertility of all life, and the ways this could inspire a shift in worldview "based on regeneration and renewal rather than domination and depletion."[10] Klein set about embodying this healing shift of worldview in herself and her body. She cut back her schedule, flew less, practised meditation, changed her diet and spent more time in the natural world to the benefit of her physical and mental wellbeing.

All natural systems, including our embodied selves, need "fallow" times of resting and rebuilding. This ecological necessity is over-ruled in capitalist industrialist cultures that promote an unearthed heroic worldview of "push harder, more often." Klein's experience of "slamming up" against biological constraints in our world and her body, taught her "a special kind of nurturing, and a constant vigilance about the limits beyond which life cannot be pushed."[11] Personal being and planetary life entwine in intricate ways. Feeling the con-nection between her nature and our world's nature, Klein learnt a wisdom and humility that supports healing for all life forms through listening to and respecting Earth's processes.

Ecological issues require us to forge conscious relationships with Earth's ecosystems. Some years ago, the eco-philosopher Thomas Berry lamented:

> We are talking only to ourselves. We are not talking to the rivers, we are not listening to the wind and stars. We have broken the great conversation. By breaking that conversation we have shattered the universe.[12]

When a conversation breaks down, misunderstandings and disconnec-tions accumulate. Then it becomes plausible and acceptable to dam and drain rivers, spray chemicals on fields, turn ravines into rubbish dumps and sacrifice mangroves for marinas. We now live within the catastrophic consequences of devastated local and regional ecosys-tems which drive climate disruption and biodiversity breakdown. We also, suggests Berry, diminish ourselves:

> Without the soaring birds, the great forests, the sounds and color-ation of the insects, the free-flowing streams, the flowering fields, the sight of clouds by day and the stars at night, we become impoverished in all that makes us human.[13]

Healing our world and ourselves requires a resumption of conversa-tions not only about, but also with, the places and beings that shape and sustains us. This brings us home to the realisation that the world is an integral part of our inner life and being.

Anthropomorphising nature is often frowned upon. But an under-standing that other forms of life are not human should not turn into a dismissal of the consciousness or communicative abilities of other beings. Or of the human need to recognise and converse with the world that forms and encompasses us. Children naturally relate to other beings with the assumption that there can be some kind of communication between them, laying down foundations for developing feelings of kinship and empathy. We do damage to ourselves and our world when we insist this is mere fantasy. "A hint of – dare I say – *animism* has entered into the scientific view" observes Barbara Ehrenreich.[14] More and more scientists are recognising the lively creativity and responsiveness of our world and her beings. Ehrenreich notes her own progression from a traditional scientific view towards a lively view of the creation, noting that:

> Once you have accepted the reality of others' human minds, you open yourself up, for better or for worse, to the possibility of still other locations for consciousness, whether in animals or in things normally thought of as "things."[15]

The possibilities this throws up for resuming and extending great conversations are endless.

Biologist David George Haskell loves trees and the songs they sing. Over many years he has studied specific trees to see how they are doing, and to understand their relationship to the places they live in and the beings who live in and around them. Haskell listens to their stories through stethoscopes and other sound detecting equipment, hearing the sounds of sap rising, larvae eating, air pockets exploding, water circulating and grasshoppers clattering. He writes that the trees' songs "tell of life's community, a net of relations" which we humans belong to "as blood kin."[16] By studying the intricate connections between trees and those who live with them and in them, Haskell has learnt about how "ecological and evolutionary tensions between cooperation and conflict are negotiated and resolved," often resulting "not in the evolution of stronger, more disconnected selves but in the dissolution of the self into relationship."[17] At a time when human evolution is approaching a possible dead end in its pursuit of individual status and satisfactions, the trees' songs point us towards a more promising evolutionary route.

Haskell's biological perspective that "life is embodied network"[18] suggests we might come to understand ourselves and our lives better through conversing with our natural world. One glorious example of conversations with trees has spontaneously arisen in Australia where residents are sending emails to some seventy thousand trees which have been mapped by number and an email address as part of the Melbourne City Council's tree maintenance program. The Council hoped mapping the trees would encourage residents to let them know about sick trees, which they did. But unexpectedly, the public started to write love letters to the trees too. These emails reveal the degree of relatedness that people feel for the branched and rooted living beings who are part of their lives. One email to a weeping myrtle reads:

> I am sitting inside near you and I noticed on the urban tree map you don't have many friends nearby. I think that's sad so I want you to know I am thinking of you.
>   I also want to thank you for providing oxygen for us to breathe in the hustle and bustle of the city.
> Best Regards
> N.

Another to a golden elm, says more simply "You deserve to be known by more than a number. I love you. Always and forever."[19] The emails reveal a powerful love for and relatedness to trees that is not commonly acknowledged or expressed in the public sphere. Modernist cultures provide few openings for people to express such feelings but when an opening occurs, a palpable desire to connect and express recognition, gratitude and care surfaces. As does an expectation that the trees will hear and respond to this human outpouring of love.

Biophilia was defined in 1984 as "the innate tendency to affiliate with life and lifelike processes" by biologist Edmund O. Wilson.[20] Biophilia expresses itself in humans through attraction to other species than our own, a need to discover and understand other life forms and the desire to relate to living creatures through metaphors and to include them in our mythologies. Exceptionalist worldviews have dismissed and repressed biophilic instincts as a matter of routine, wounding ourselves and our world. To liberate these instincts, we need to feel and respond to these wounds in a personal way, as well as understand them from a biological and cultural perspectives. When we can initiate and maintain great and small conversations with our natural world, we live better, feel better, learn better and heal better.[21]

Widening the frame

An ecological self develops as much through other-discovery as self-discovery. The possibilities of this are endless and the emotional stretch challenging, especially within the context of global heating. Finding out more about myself and how I live through understanding why glaciers are melting, jellyfish are multiplying and hurricanes are strengthening is astonishing, disturbing and enlightening. To take it in and care about it, I have to entirely rework the notion of who I think I am and what the nature of life is. There is much to love in what I am learning about the world and my existence within it. Even in the midst of my grief over ecological destructions, I feel a joy in this growing appreciation of the wonders of our planet.

To be able to live in relationship with the depth and complexity of our world, we need to embrace ecological understandings about who we are. Carl Jung described the process of surrendering egocentric perspectives to an experience of one's self being part of a larger whole as *the relativisation of the ego*. This surrender can feel like a symbolic death. Biologically and symbolically, death is part of a larger transformative process. Climate engagement can bring a radical reassessment of identity, meaning and power because it encourages a more conscious encounter with systemic complexity, biological finiteness and death. As this happens, conditioned attitudes, beliefs and goals unravel.

The larger work of becoming ourselves and forging our own conscious values, while holding an awareness of the universal nature of life, was called *individuation* by Jung. He described this maturing process as becoming true to one's self in a way that "does not shut out from the world, but gathers the world to oneself."[22] This allows a more authentic, complex and flexible sense of self to emerge which recognises both individual uniqueness, and commonality with others, as well as the larger, mostly unconscious, dimensions of ourselves and our world.

This widening of the frame, and relativising of ego is an ongoing process. Changing consciousness is not a fast train with fixed stations. Mostly it's a slow and meandering walk, with occasional switchbacks and chaotic interludes. I find I can have moments of intense ecological awareness and connection, while at other times I can feel disconnected and encased in my own self-centred bubble. Much of the time, I feel caught somewhere between these two modes of consciousness. What else can I expect? These are chrysalis times when many of us feel in transition between worn-out forms and barely recognisable new ones. But the knowledge of my embeddedness within an ecological world is increasingly becoming part of my life and being, in humbling and surprising ways. Once I had assumed my most significant relationships would be with humans, not beaches, trees, rocks, cats, kookaburras and termites. But what I have learnt, is that the relational knowing that psychotherapy cherishes as a way of developing consciousness and nurturing meaning, can be experienced as much with Earth as with people. Who knew? The answer is very many people, for a very long time.

For millennia, Indigenous cultures have lived and continue to live within cosmologies of kinship with Earth and her beings. And then there are other naturalists who for centuries have been loving and learning about Earth, following trails of connections across lands and seas, through forests and marshes; while nature-immersed poets, philosophers and mystics across the globe have long celebrated the natural world and human embeddedness within it. In every culture, there are always people who have related to animals as significant others, while most children experience strong bonds with their pets and special places. Given all of this, the depth of ecological disconnectedness in contemporary cultures as a result of industrialisation, colonisation and urbanisation is deeply shocking.

As the climate crisis spurs existential discussions about who we are, what matters most, and what keeps us alive, egos become relativised and worldviews less "humanised." At the same time such a massive re-visioning of human being and agency arouses collective resistance, partly because it signals a death of identity as well as of worldview. For some people, the climate crisis is a catalyst to become even more exceptionalist in their thinking through geo-engineering solutions, or fantastical plans for escape to other planets. While it is possible that some geo-engineering interventions (such as seeding oceans with iron or spraying aerosol particles into the atmosphere) may, with enormous amounts of luck, buy some time and lives in the short run, they literally risk life on Earth. Large-scale human interventions working across, and even against, ecosystems perpetuate modernist disconnections and denials in their attempts to control the uncontrollable. In some cases they attempt to shape the world for the endless economic and population growth which capitalism demands, and which the Earth cannot sustain. Exceptionalist fantasies bolster narcissistic perspectives, quashing unsettling questions, inconvenient truths and the frightening enormity and inevitability of unintended consequences. This approach cheats people from developing a maturity that can learn from and commit to the interactive dance of life on Earth.

By contrast, Project Drawdown, pioneered by Paul Hawken, provides one hundred systemic solutions that if taken together could reverse global heating by drawing carbon dioxide out of the atmosphere. One core principle of this Project is learning how to collaborate with "the helpers, those microbes, plants and animals that do the daily alchemy of turning carbon into life."[23] Hawken's approach is an integrative one weaving connections between individual actions, social organisation, economic outcomes and ecosystems. Regenerative agriculture figures strongly, along with other systemic solutions such as educating girls, reducing food waste, protecting tropical forests and creating walkable cities. These kinds of solutions help to remedy the disconnections of contemporary thinking and living. While many employ cutting-edge technologies, they nearly all have reference points in sustainable practices evolved within traditional cultures. Increasingly, ecologists and many others are recognising the importance of listening to and learning from First Nations' peoples whose worldviews never lost their nature connectedness or conversational ways with all of our Earth kin.

Respecting Indigenous knowing

One sign that ecological consciousness is in the process of evolving, writes Tim Winton, is the way that "the environment has started to make the kinds of claims upon us that perhaps only family can."[24] For Indigenous people, this experience of kinship with Earth is the basis of human life. Earth-centred Indigenous worldviews are grounded in systems of relationship and reciprocity that recognise human dependency on, and commonality with, all forms of life on Earth. Ethnobiologist and ecological anthropologist Felice Wyndham observes how many Indigenous peoples are trained to use "a form of enhanced mindfulness" which can intimately sense the world by tuning into viewpoints and perspectives of other beings including rocks, water and clouds.[25] This enhanced cognitive ability is highly sensitive to the complex interconnections between species and ecosystems. It is a knowledge which is held and passed on through cultural practices of storytelling, singing, dancing, dreaming, practising rituals and performing ceremonies.

Traditional Ecological Knowledge (TEK) offers key teachings and leadership for healing the harms that modernist cultures have caused through their adversarial and exploitative approaches to our natural world. Botanist Robin Wall Kimmerer observes that Western science excludes emotion and aesthetic responses.[26] As a member of the Citizen Potawatomi Nation, Kimmerer suggests ways in which Indigenous worldviews can extend scientific understandings to address issues of ecological ethics and values. For a start, she challenges the use of "it" as a pronoun for any life form, including Earth, because it disrespects, objectifies and distances ourselves from our fellow beings.[27] Kimmerer explains that understanding our world as animate opens the way to developing reciprocal relations that oblige us to sustain the Earth that sustains us. An important part of being human, she suggests, is to be educated about the gifts each of us carries and can give on behalf of our community and land, in return for the gift of life. Her own gift she believes is to integrate Indigenous knowledge into science education so that scientists and ecologists can draw on a plurality of understandings and approaches.[28]

Indigenous knowledge is transmitted through many forms including stories, dreams and the reverie between waking and sleeping. "This is when we can tap into the deep knowledge all around us, not just the surface," says Gladys Milroy, a Palyku elder from the Pilbara region of Australia.[29] Working together with her daughter Jill Milroy, they write:

> For Aboriginal people, the land is full of stories, and we are born from our Mother the land, into these stories. The old people tell us stories that nurture and sustain us through life ... It is the birthright of all Aboriginal children to be born into the right story. Indeed, it is the birthright and greatest gift we can give all children. The right story connects us intimately to our country, giving us our place and our identity. The right story embeds us deeply in nature, connected to the living spirit.[30]

Milroy and Milroy describe colonising peoples like the British as "story nomads" who:

> wander about in other people's stories, mucking them up and changing the endings; disbelieving most, stealing some, selling others. They often come too late to understand what the story is about, starting in the middle of a story but claiming it is the beginning. They may leave before the end, so they don't have to face the consequences of broken stories. They are the perpetual travellers of the story world because they have "disremembered"

their own stories, consigning them to myth, mysticism, religion, allegory, metaphor or narrative: the "not quite true" category.[31]

First Nation's people, and their supporters, campaign not only for the restitution of their lands and cultural rights but for a universal recognition and valuing of Earth-centred stories. These wisdom stories about the necessity and beauty of maintaining respectful connections with "all our relations" are increasingly finding expression in contemporary Indigenous arts and literature while films such as *Whale Rider*, *Moana* and *Avatar* show what living with Earth as kin sounds like, looks like and feels like to audiences who are far removed from such teachings.

Indigenous cultures are on the frontline of experiencing climate catastrophes. At climate conferences and campaigns they lead the way, physically and morally, in their expression of grief, outrage and commitment to ecological restoration based on respect for Earth's processes and traditional knowledge. What they also teach is how collective expressions of love, loss and grief can fuel passionate and determined campaigns. In 2012, a small Pacific archipelago called Tokelau became the first nation in the world to make the switch to 100% renewable energy, beginning its ongoing campaign against the use of fossil fuels worldwide.

Tokelau has made an alliance with fourteen other Pacific Island nations to form the Pacific Climate Warriors, under the banner of "We are not drowning. We are fighting."[32] They have built traditional canoes and sailed them to a blockade of the coal port in Newcastle, Australia and campaigned globally for the cessation of fossil fuels and other forms of climate action, challenging the media's portrayal of them as helpless victims. The courage and stamina of the Pacific Climate Warriors is paralleled in other Indigenous-led campaigns across the world, including the Stop Dakota Access Pipeline and the Amazon Alliance. Their campaigns are powered by the knowledge that the lands they live on are an integral part of who they are, giving them a fierce spirit and commitment to protect their places and communities.

The difference between the proactive responses of Indigenous communities to climate disruption and the inertia of modern societies is great. When people's cultural stories don't recognise their belonging in, and dependency on the world, they lack ability to articulate feelings of diminishment and loss when the ecologies they live in are destroyed. By contrast, Indigenous stories are skilled in attuning people to the changes and losses of the ecosystems they live within, and acting in response. The climate emergency is acting as a spur for Indigenous communities to extend this cultural knowledge to the world. Anne Poelina, a Nyikina Traditional Custodian from the Kimberly region of Australia and academic researcher, describes how the life of her people is lived "in a deep circular storytelling relationship with nature, planet earth and humanity"[33] which bestows legitimacy, cultural heritage rights and responsibilities. In her view "This responsibility now extends to fellow Australians, and indeed and through our actions to fellow world citizens."[34] Poelina's view is echoed by Rangimarie Turuki Rose Pere, a Māori educator and elder, who teaches that "We've come to a place where we're all in it together, we can no longer separate ourselves from each other. It's a time of unity, a time for the indigenous wisdom-keepers to share our knowledge with the rest of the world."[35] Teachings like this are evolving new stories that analyse the ecological and social traumas inflicted by colonisation while seeking to address them through cultural practices and dialogues.

One of the most successful examples of cultural evolution and healing stimulated through Indigenous and non-Indigenous dialogues has taken place in Aotearoa New Zealand. While early British colonialism widely dismissed and repressed Māori culture, in recent times, Aotearoa has become a robust bicultural nation. Māori land rights are recognised and the Government and other public institutions, including schools, incorporate Māori protocols and language. Recent Māori campaigns have successfully achieved the recognition of the legal status of personhood for both the Te Urewera National Park and the Whanganui River.[36]

The lead negotiator for the Whanganui *iwi* (tribe), Gerrard Albert explained that they consider the river as an ancestor, an indivisible whole.[37] Finding a way to approximate this in law so others can understand and work with the river similarly, liberates Whanganui River from colonising concepts of ownership and management. It is not an inherently anti-development or anti-economic stance, says Albert. Instead it establishes the central belief of the river as a living entity whose welfare must be considered for all future use.[38] Rather than being discouraged by the differences between *Pakeha* (European) culture and their own, the *iwi* are finding ways to express Māori beliefs through Pakeha institutions, such as the legal system. This is cultural evolution at work that has buoyed the international Earth jurisprudence movement's efforts to win recognition of the legal rights of other places around the world.[39]

Ongoing cultural exchanges between Māori and Pakeha in Aotearoa look both backward and forward in evolving beliefs, values and practices that respect ecosystems, and nurture people's relationships within them. Just as with the reconciliation processes in South Africa following the abolition of apartheid, these cultural dialogues recognise the necessity for truth telling, expressions of guilt and grief, heartfelt apologies and reparation work. This deep work of listening and dialogue transforms worldviews and social relations. The conservative New Zealand society I grew up in fifty years ago, is nothing like the vibrant culture of Aotearoa of today. Assimilationist policies have given way to bicultural initiatives founded upon both the recognition of Māori values and the harms of colonisation. Out of this process, has emerged robust speech and evolving practices that recognise the necessity and beauty of living in good relations with Earth and respecting Indigenous knowledge. Aotearoa is at the forefront of global climate action, with a carbon pricing scheme, a ban on new offshore oil drilling and a commitment to be carbon neutral by 2050. Cultural evolution in Aotearoa, based on listening to Indigenous worldviews and reviewing Western-based ones, points the way ahead for all contemporary societies. Human cultures cannot hope to survive, let alone thrive, without respecting Indigenous wisdoms about our kinship with Earth, with their love and care for our common ground.

Cherishing our young

Young children start life with an instinctive affinity for our natural world, readily seeking out the company of animals, birds, trees, rocks, shells and places as their special companions and friends. Indigenous cultures nurture and encourage this affinity, recognising it as central to a child's wellbeing, identity and survival. Gladys & Jill Milroy write:

> All Australian children deserve to know the country that they share through the stories that Aboriginal people can tell them and through the different ways of knowing country. This is what gives children the feathers to fly with the birds and grow with the trees.[40]

Physically experiencing our world, through encounters with tadpoles, wind, rock pools, caves, ants, or autumn leaves, weaves children into the larger life of the world. These encounters arouse children's primal curiosity and feelings of relatedness to Earth. When cultures support children's development with nature-based teaching stories they support lifelong practices of observing and caring for our world.

Children's birthright to traditional stories and embodied knowledge of our natural world has been eroded in recent generations, as Richard Louv charts in his ground-breaking book *Last Child in the Woods*.[41] Privatisation, urbanisation, digitalisation, ecological destructions and education and parenting practices all contribute to what Louv describes as *nature deficit disorder* and the extinction of outdoor life. The latest editions of the *Oxford Junior Dictionary* mirror, and possibly contribute to, children's increasing nature disconnection, by dropping words such as almond, apricot, goldfish, heron, ivy, lavender and leopard from their pages.[42] The words that replace them in the dictionary, such as blog, broadband, celebrity, chatroom and vandalism, do not conjure up a happier or healthier childhood.[43]

Risk-averse societies contribute to this problem by discouraging outdoor play and adventure. But what use protecting children from the dangers of forests when the disappearance of forests are risking all of our lives? Rosemary Randall suggests risk-averse societies are unconsciously compensating for their lack of environmental care.[44] There is a painful irony in modern societies obsessively micromanaging risk, particularly in children's lives, while failing to take responsibility for the alarming risks of climate disruption. The unintended consequence of cocooning children from risks, including outdoor play and adventure, is that it makes them less resilient in a climate-disrupted world that is becoming ever more at risk.

Despite all of this, or perhaps because all of this, some young people are becoming very passionate about speaking up about the risks and losses of climate crisis. In August 2018, a fifteen-year-old Swedish school girl called Greta Thunberg dropped out of her classes to protest outside the gates of the Swedish Government about lack of effective climate action. The flyers she handed out read "I am doing this because you adults are shitting on my future." She asked why she should go to school when "Facts don't matter anymore, politicians aren't listening to the scientists, so why should I learn?"[45] When I first read about Thunberg, I admired her grittiness, determination and desire for truth telling. But looking at her photo, I felt very sad seeing her small figure and placard hunched against the railings of the Swedish Parliament.

I sensed her feelings of abandonment in a world where adults are not acting to ensure her generation's future livelihood and wellbeing. But, within a few months, Greta's protest had gathered momentum, inspiring student strikes across the world. The student strike I attended in Sydney in November 2018 was electrifying with its passionate speeches and furious placards. It moved me and many other adults in ways that no other protest had. A number of young children I spoke to told me they were here because they felt so sad about the extinction of animals. The teenager speakers had an impressive grasp of climate science and politics, declaring themselves to be "the generation that cannot wait until it's too late."

Shortly after this, Greta Thunberg challenged leaders at the UN COP24 climate conference by saying, "You say you love your children above all else, and yet you are stealing their future in front of their very eyes … We have come here to let you know that change is coming, whether you like it or not."[46]

Protesting school students are acutely aware of the disjuncture between the adult world's rhetoric of care for children, and the actual consequences of not taking strong climate action now. They also know that their passion and truth telling cuts through adult disavowals. At the far larger student rally in March 2019, I saw placards reading "we are acting as adults, because you are not," "we must do it," "oceans are rising and so are we," "march now or swim later." What was on display was the steely determination for the fight for their lives and a clear-sighted fear of the consequences of not acting.

Students taking climate action are creating their own initiation into adulthood in reaction to cultures that are too immature and irresponsible to safeguard the future for their young. In doing so, the students are facing into climate fears and griefs that many adults are distancing themselves from. In the United States, a group of young people is appealing to the legal system to hold the Government accountable for its lack of responsibility to younger generations in providing a safe future. They are suing the Government for failing to act on climate change in a lawsuit named *Juliana v U.S.* Environmental law professor, Mary Wood describes this lawsuit as "the biggest case on the planet."[47] It has already scored significant victories and sparked a wave of similar suits in other countries. Upholding the case for trial, Anne Aiken, a District Court Judge, wrote:

> I have no doubt that the right to a climate system capable of sustaining human life is fundamental to a free and ordered

society ... Just as marriage is the foundation of the family, a stable climate system is quite literally the foundation of society, without which there would be neither civilization nor progress.[48]

While key adult supporters have ensured that this case proceeds in the face of opposition from the Trump Government, it is the children's stories, emotions and presence that create the means to acknowledge the graveness and immediacy of climate disruption. Miko Vergun, a sixteen-year-old from Oregon, fears not being able to visit her native Marshall Islands before the islands sink beneath rising seas. Other young complainants speak of the deadly effects of flooding, ocean acidification and warmer temperatures on their home environments, vividly spelling out the consequences of inaction by the time they will reach middle age.

Trying to hide news of the climate crisis from children once they are past a very young age is neither possible nor desirable. The best that parents and teachers can do is to talk to young people in ways that acknowledge the urgency of the situation while highlighting solutions, encouraging active responses and embodying love and appreciation for Earth. The psychological wellbeing of children and young people is highly dependent on the emotional honesty, wisdom and stamina of adults around them. Adults need to face into their own climate fears and griefs to be able to fully listen to young people's feelings and thoughts about climate disruption and join with them in climate action. Greta Thunberg's stern statement to the leaders at Davos – "I don't want you to be hopeful. I want you to panic. I want you to feel the fear I feel every day. And then I want you to act"[49] – is a call out for all adults to endure emotional pain with, and on behalf, of younger generations.

Young people are stepping up to be at the forefront of cultural change in response to climate disruption because their lives depend on it. Their direct words and outpourings of fear, grief and determination is piercing adult denials, stirring conscience and consciousness. Their heartfelt expressions of love for threatened species and natural places help all of us to reconnect, revalue and re-story what has been devalued and deadened. In Indigenous cultures rites of passage for young people have traditionally involved strengthening ties with our natural world. By understanding young people's engagement with climate disruption as a necessary collective rite of passage, not just for them but for all of us, we can acknowledge and encourage the ways this is birthing feelings of purpose, belonging and identity grounded in ecological consciousness. The advocacy and insight of young people protesting climate disruption can lead and empower us all, if we choose to listen.

Connecting personal to collective

Climate action depends on and develops the power of the collective. As people join initiatives to set up renewable energy projects, halt fracking, clean up oceans, regenerate forests, protect rivers, lobby for divestment and take direct action, they transform themselves and their communities. "We are called to assist the Earth to heal her wounds and in the process heal our own" declared Wangiri Maathai when she won the Nobel Prize in 2004 for her work with the Green Belt Movement in Kenya. This Movement analyses the ways that environmental degradation, deforestation and food insecurity are driven by systemic issues of disempowerment, disenfranchisement and a loss of traditional values.[50] Its remedies are holistic, combining citizen and environmental education programmes, tree planting projects, campaigns to save forests and lobbying for political accountability. One of their major initiatives teaches poor rural women an understanding of the larger causes of their problems, from ecological ones such as deforestation and desertification through to corrupt governance and the injustices of globalisation. This knowledge empowers women to plant trees and lobby for political change and economic justice for themselves and their communities.

Ecological destructions caused by humans need to be addressed systemically. The Green Belt Movement's holistic approach intertwines biological, economic, psychological and political education with hands-on campaigns for tree planting and the preservations of forests. In the process of learning to hold their political leaders accountable, women develop capacities for leadership and initiating cultural change. Calling upon traditional cultural values of pulling together (known as *the harambee spirit*), the Green Belt Movement has not only succeeded in planting more than fifty-one million trees and saving public spaces and forests, it has also supported women's education, the alleviation of poverty, community empowerment and Kenya's transition to democracy.[51] Today its work continues to evolve across four interlinked themes of tree planting and watershed protection, gender livelihood and advocacy, climate change and mainstream advocacy, providing a role model for other integrated programmes across the world.

Restoring connections and collaborations between individuals, communities and ecosystems is crucial for climate action. This is especially so in neoliberal societies which socially condition people into being isolated bystanders rather than engaged participants in community life. People who are socialised into a narrow focus on personal success through endless competition and comparison become blinded to the world, and much of their own natural capacities. As a consequence, feelings of numbness, emptiness and loneliness ramp up while feelings of belonging, authenticity and compassion fail to develop. In her analysis of the neoliberal "culture of uncare," psychoanalyst Sally Weintrobe observes the way that this culture uses "any argument and any means to keep me in the uncaring dissociated mindset, split off from the part of me that cares."[52] It is a mindset that encourages destructive patterns of consumption through appealing to greed and feelings of entitlement, while hiding or dismissing the associated ecological, social and psychological costs, as we explore further in the next chapter.

Addressing false cultural beliefs and the damage they cause is something we need to do with others, for support, comfort and collaborative truth telling. Compassionate and tolerant dialogues are crucial in helping people to identify a sense of something being not right in themselves and their world, and then to reflect on what is needed in response. Hearing others struggle with similar feelings and experiences lays the way for negotiating the conflicted feelings and thoughts that we all carry, and which become more highlighted in times of change. A basic premise of depth psychology is that identifying suppressed thoughts and feelings begins the work of healing. Acknowledge feelings of sadness about dying fish, or anxiety about a heatwave deepens understandings and mobilises energy for action, when done in the company of supportive others.

One vital learning in relation to climate crisis, is that although we are not individually to blame, we need to take responsibility for meaningful action within a systemic worldview. Making the shift from focusing on climate disruption as the fault of particular individuals or groups, rather than as an outcome of systemic values and exchanges, supports the transition from disengaged bystander to engaged participant. By grappling together with the dilemmas and possibilities of climate action, we begin the process of reimagining ourselves as ecologically responsible human beings, capable of empathy and restraint.

One woman inspired by the possibilities of linking social and ecological action with consciousness change is Katerina Gaita, a climate change communicator from Melbourne, Australia. After reading Philip Sutton and David Spratt's book, *Climate Code Red: The Case for Emergency Action*, she cried for months, waking up at night with wet cheeks. She remembers the "strange loneliness that comes from being amongst other people who aren't feeling the same grief that you are."[53] Her experience inspired Gaita to find a way to provide emotional support and practical opportunities for collaborative action for other people connecting to climate issues. She recognises that while you can raise people's awareness through media campaigns, it takes extended, in-depth conversations to help people really come to terms with the climate crisis and decide how to respond to it. To create a space for such conversation, Gaita founded Climate for Change, an initiative that facilitates social gatherings to discuss the climate disruption and support people becoming active participants in social and political change.

At Climate for Change gatherings, attendees watch a video about climate change and then pair up to talk about their feelings in response. A group conversation follows about what changes are needed and the ways individuals can help to create systemic change. Gaita observes that at times dinner guests do struggle "to see themselves as citizens, rather than individuals or consumers" but generally "they're relieved to be able to think and talk about this in a meaningful and constructive way."[54] Generally people leave more hopeful, having learnt skills for opening up climate conversations with friends and family, as well as pledging to social actions such as writing to politicians, hosting a gathering or training as a facilitator. Since 2014 Climate for Change has facilitated more than 600 conversations with over 6000 participants,[55] demonstrating that people do have an appetite for talking and acting on climate issues when given space, support and a meaningful context.

Bringing people together to engage with the causes and wounds of climate disruption is as much psychological work as it is ecological, cultural and political work. It needs to be done with respect, care and a willingness for deep listening, to ourselves, each other and the world. This requires establishing a safe space for exploratory dialogues, which gives people permission to speak honestly without fear of criticism or negative repercussions. When people name what has been repressed or outlawed from cultural consciousness, it can arouse defensive and hostile reactions from others, and even within ourselves at times. Acknowledging the ways in which lies, injustice and exploitation have been tolerated as social norms is a confronting process. It is much eased, however, when we can share the conflicted and distressed feelings that arise and understand them as an inevitable part of personal and social transformation.

It takes ongoing collaborative efforts to dismantle established cultural divides, denials and false beliefs, and to form worldviews that integrate what has been suppressed. The Women's Liberation Movement provides one example of how this process can be facilitated. Throughout the sixties and seventies, large groups of women met in *consciousness raising* groups in order to challenge cultural beliefs that maintained false truths about women's weakness and inferiority to men. These groups acted as social containers for psychological and cultural change. Within them women supported one another to retrieve exiled or tabooed knowledge, while evolving new cultural models of gender identity and equality that aimed to increase the wellbeing of both women and men. Meetings were often tumultuous as women disputed entrenched notions of identity and named feelings and understandings that had been long denied in patriarchal culture. Deep listening, tolerance and collaboration were all essential for constructing more nuanced and complex views about gender relations and identity. So too was emotional support to deal with the inevitable pushbacks from men and women resistant to change. Today this consciousness change is well under way, although by no means complete. For the millennial generation of both sexes, there is an ease of acceptance about the fluidity of gender and its roles, which is dismantling split and fixed views, along with an increased willingness to call out sexual inequalities and exploitation.

For a new consciousness to evolve there needs to be progression beyond idealised fantasies of creating a mirror opposite of the old view, which is in itself another form of denial. For example, some early feminist thought fantasised about establishing matriarchal societies that relegated men to secondary positions, or even obliteration. However, over time, these compensatory fantasies gave way to fairer and more realistic imaginings about how to deal with the complexities of re-visioning gender identities and negotiating gender equalities. Similarly, compensatory environmental fantasies might envision banishing technologies, or even the human species, as a way of pursuing an idyllic world. Such fantasies often idealise ecosystems as static and harmonious, while demonising humans. In effect, they seek to bypass the uncertainties and disorders of human–ecological relations and the risks of learning to negotiate them. When conscious-ness change evolves beyond compensatory visions, its analysis and imaginings become more complex and less idealised. In the case of ecological consciousness, this means evolving systemic approaches that extend beyond blanket or "magic bullet" solutions.

Ecological consciousness can only evolve through a complex pro-cess of experiencing grief over ecological losses and destructions, identifying their multiple causes and effects, analysing contributing cultural beliefs such as human exceptionalism, experimenting with collaborative practices for restoration and cultivating collective com-passion and creativity. We cannot meet the challenges of the climate crisis short-sightedly or in the short term. It demands a long view and an expansive understanding of life. Narrow and singular approaches decimate ecosystems. We need inclusive visions and sys-temic actions to remedy the single-minded pursuits of the modern age and capitalist and expansionist economies.

As the climate emergency cracks the walls of modernist world-views, it reveals a dazzling array of interconnections never witnessed before. Consciously participating in and celebrating this creative interplay of the world is vital for human survival. In the next two chapters we deep dive into the psychological dimensions of climate action, while the concluding chapter explores the creative power of emerging collective myths, dreams and imaginings in response to ecological crisis.

Notes

1 Seed, J. (2005). The ecological self. *Earth Light Magazine #53* 14 (4). Retrieved from https://earthlight.org/2005/essay53_johnseed.html
2 Haskell, D. G. (2017). *The song of trees: Stories from nature's great con-nectors.* Melbourne, Australia: Black Inc., p. 18.
3 Bright, B. & Marshall, J. (2019). *Multi-logue on the cultural complex of the English speaking west. Earth climate dreams: Dialogues with depth psychologists in the Age of the Anthropocene.* Honolulu, HI: Depth Insights.
4 Seed, J. (2005). The ecological self. *Earth Light Magazine #53* 14 (4). Retrieved from https://earthlight.org/2005/essay53_johnseed.html
5 Rust, M-J. (2012). Ecological intimacy. In M-J. Rust & N. Tottton (Eds.), *Vital signs: Psychological responses to ecological crisis.* London, UK: Karnac, pp. 152–153.
6 Key, D. & Kerr, M. (2012). The natural change project. In M-J. Rust & N. Totton (Eds.), *Vital signs.* London, UK: Karnac, p. 241.

7 Key, D. & Kerr, M. (2012). The natural change project. In M-J. Rust &
   N. Totton (Eds.), *Vital signs*. London, UK: Karnac, pp. 249–250.
8 Klein, N. (2014). *This changes everything: Capitalism vs. climate*.
   New York, NY: Simon & Schuster, p. 423.
9 Ibid, p. 427.
10 Ibid, p. 424.
11 Ibid, p. 442.
12 Berry, T. Retrieved from www.earthheart.org/url/berry.htm
13 Berry, T. (2011). *The great work: Our way into the future*. Camarthen,
   UK: Crown, p. 200.
14 Ehrenreich, B. (2014). *Living with a wild God*. London, UK: Granta,
   p. 233.
15 Ibid., pp. 218–219.
16 Haskell, D. G. (2017). *The song of trees: Stories from nature's great con-
   nectors*. Melbourne, Australia: Black Inc., p. ix.
17 Ibid, p. x.
18 Ibid.
19 Melbourne City Council media release, confirmed by personal
   communication.
20 Wilson, E. O. (2006). *The creation: An appeal to save life on Earth*.
   New York, NY: Norton, p. 63.
21 See Kellert, S. R. (2012). *Birthright: people and nature in the modern
   world*. New Haven, CT: Taale University Press for an array of research
   into the benefits of human-nature relations.
22 Jung, C. G. (1969). *The structure and dynamics of the psyche* (2nd ed.
   CW Vol. 8). London, UK: Routledge & Kegan Paul, p. 226.
23 Benyus, J. (2017). Reciprocity. In P. Hawken (Ed.), *Drawdown: The
   most comprehensive plan ever proposed to reverse global warming*.
   New York, NY: Penguin, p. 215.
24 Winton, T. (2015). *Island home: A landscape memoir*. London, UK:
   Hamish Hamilton, p. 110.
25 Robbins, J. (2018, Apr 26). Native knowledge: What ecologists are learning from Indigenous people. Yale Environment 360. Retrieved from
   https://e360.yale.edu/features
26 Kimmerer, R. W. (2018). The intelligence in all kinds of life. On being
   with Krista Tippett. Retrieved from https://onbeing.org/programs/robin-
   wall-kimmerer-the-intelligence-in-all-kinds-of-life/
27 Ibid.
28 Ibid.
29 Milroy, G. I. & Milroy, J. (2008). Different ways of knowing: Trees are
   our families too. In S. Morgan, T. Mia & B. Kwaymullina (Eds.), *Heart-
   sick for country: Stories of love, spirit and creation*. Fremantle, Australia:
   Fremantle Press, p. 22.
30 Ibid, p. 24.
31 Ibid, p. 29.
32 Maiava, M. (2013, Mar 4). Pacific warriors. Retrieved from www
   .oxfam.org.au/2013/03/pacific-warriors/
33 Poelina, A. (2016, Aug 12). Blood line song line Pt. 2. Retrieved from
   https://greataustralianstory.com.au/story/blood-line-song-line-pt2

34 Ibid.
35 Browdy, J. (2015, Mar 2). When the grandmothers awoke. *Yes Magazine.*
    www.yesmagazine.org/issues/together-with-earth/when-the-grandmothers-
    awoke
36 Daley, M. (2017, Mar 16). Whanganui river gets the rights of a legal
    person. Retrieved from www.stuff.co.nz/national/politics/90488008/Whan
    ganui-River-gets-the-rights-of-a-legal-person
37 Roy, E. A. (2017, Mar 16). New Zealand river granted same legal rights
    as human being. *The Guardian.* Retrieved from www.theguardian.com
    /world/2017/mar/16/new-zealand-river-granted-same-legal-rights-as-
    human-being
38 Roy, E. A. (2017, Mar 16). New Zealand river granted same legal rights
    as human being. *The Guardian.* Retrieved from www.theguardian.com
    /world/2017/mar/16/new-zealand-river-granted-same-legal-rights-as-
    human-being
39 Lee, D. (2017, Nov 8). Indigenous perspectives at the forefront of environ-
    mental jurisprudence. Retrieved from www.earthlawcenter.org/blog-entries
    /2017/11/indigenous-perspectives-at-the-forefront-of-environmental-
    jurisprudence
40 Milroy, G. I. & Milroy, J. (2008). Different ways of knowing: Trees are
    our families too. In S. Morgan, T. Mia & B. Kwaymullina (Eds.), *Heart-
    sick for country: Stories of love, spirit and creation.* Fremantle, Australia:
    Fremantle Press, p. 42.
41 Louv, R. (2010). *The last child in the woods: Saving our children from
    nature deficit disorder.* London, UK: Atlantic Books.
42 Flood, A. (2015, Jan 13). Oxford Junior Dictionary's replacement of
    "natural" words with 21st-century terms sparks outcry. *The Guardian.*
    Retrieved from www.theguardian.com/books/2015/jan/13/oxford-junior-
    dictionary-replacement-natural-words
43 Brown, A. (2008, Dec 10). Goodbye herons, hello celebrity. *The Guard-
    ian.* Retrieved from www.theguardian.com/commentisfree/2008/dec/10/
    oxford-junior-dictionary
44 Randall, R. (2005). A new climate for psychotherapy? *Psychotherapy
    and Politics International 3* (3), 165–179.
45 Crouch, D. (2018, Sep 1). The Swedish 15-year-old who's cutting class
    to fight the climate crisis. *The Guardian.* Retrieved from www
    .theguardian.com/science/2018/sep/01/swedish-15-year-old-cutting-class-
    to-fight-the-climate-crisis
46 Thunberg, G. (2019). No one is too small to make a difference. London,
    UK: Penguin Books, pp. 15–16.
47 Parker, L. (2018, Nov 9). "Biggest case on the planet" pits kids vs. cli-
    mate change. *National Geographic.* Retrieved from https://news
    .nationalgeographic.com/2017/03/kids-sue-us-government-climate-change/
48 Ibid.
49 Thunberg, G. (2019). No one is too small to make a difference. London,
    UK: Penguin Books, p. 24.
50 Our history Retrieved from www.greenbeltmovement.org/who-we-are
    /our-history

51 The green belt movement: 40 Years of impact. (2018, Mar 21). Retrieved from www.goldmanprize.org/blog/green-belt-movement-wangari-maathai/

52 Weintrobe, S. (2015, Dec 2). A new imagination. Retrieved from www .climatepsychologyalliance.org/explorations/papers/103-anew-imagination

53 Miller, G. (2016, Nov 7). Climate change meets party plans as activists organise dinners to save the planet. *Earshot*. Retrieved from www .abc.net.au/news/2016-11-07/climate-change-activists-organise-dinners-to-save-the-planet/7992282

54 Ibid.

55 Who we are. Retrieved January 2019 from www.climateforchange.org.au /about

Chapter 5

Tending to daily life

Surfacing tensions

Like many people, I feel daily tensions about how to live responsibly from an ecological point of view. The climate emergency provokes many unsettling questions about what is "the good life," especially if you live in a prosperous country with high carbon emission lifestyles. It is challenging to make the connection between driving cars and creeping deserts, meat eating and coral reef bleaching, air conditioners and melting glaciers. New ethical dilemmas surface which are often out of synch with older moralities and values. "How often should I fly to visit my ageing parents? Do I give my sick friend the imported flowers she loves? Should I buy new energy efficient appliances when my old ones work well?" Old and new imperatives collide, as the norms of contemporary lifestyles conflict with developing ecological sensitivities.

Trying to resolve all the daily dilemmas thrown up by the climate crisis is impossible on an individual basis. The major determinants of so many parameters and influences in life are the social, economic and political systems that we live within. Techno-industrialist economies run on high levels of fossil-fuelled growth and consumption. Here in Australia, I can lower my personal carbon footprint somewhat by choosing to use public transport, eat locally produced foods, compost leftovers, install solar panels and so on. This joins the dots between what I know about climate disruption and how I live, helping to reduce the strain of cognitive dissonance. The larger piece of the emissions story, however, is determined by governmental and corporate decisions about carbon pricing, transport infrastructure, land clearing practices, mining licences, and which energy producers get subsidised and supported. So my individual agency is limited even although my awareness and concern is high.

Frustrations, however, can be very productive. Climate crisis tensions are pushing people to rethink their ideas about personal agency, social action and political processes. As a result, the neoliberal ideology that has held sway in much of the developed world for the last forty years is coming under increasing scrutiny. Its central tenets of privatisation, deregulation, tax cuts and free trade deals have empowered corporations to make enormous profits at high costs to ecosystems, social equity and emotional wellbeing. Margaret Thatcher, a torch bearer for neoliberalism, famously declared there is no such thing as society. This downgrading of social good for free market principles has in many ways paved the way for a "culture of uncare"[1] where citizens are treated as isolated individuals and rebranded as consumers rather than active citizens. Those with wealth can place their bid for symbolic immortality as a person of lasting status through accumulating material goods and social power. But for most people, societies and our planet, the neoliberal construction of personal identity and purpose does not work well or bring happiness. A person who depends on consumerism for a sense of self is fragile and easily manipulated through inner feelings of emptiness and lack of self-worth. Individualism weakens the fabric of social connections, breeds loneliness and falsifies ecological realities.

But now there is a significant pushback under way. The climate crisis is especially proving to be a significant catalyst for calling out some of the destructive consequences of neoliberal policies and practices, including revelations about the way neoliberal think tanks have generated significant opposition to climate science and action. Climate disruption, and our responses to it, reveals the interconnections between climate, atmosphere and oceans, between humans, ecosystems and economies, and between individuals, social movements and political responsiveness. Making these connections helps us to understand how we are active participants in the ecological and social systems that shape us, and that we can shape through collective action. As anthropologist Jonathan Marshall points out:

> human beings are complex systems embedded in social systems which are complex systems, in family systems which are complex systems, in ecological systems which are complex systems, in a global system which is a complex system … whatever you do is a form of activism.[2]

A systemic worldview shows that while individual changes may appear limited in terms of climate action, they matter a great deal when perceived through a systemic lens. Or, as the fortune cookie I received last night at a Chinese restaurant read, "A snow flake rarely thinks it's responsible for the avalanche."

While one person's actions may not achieve much singly, when joined to the actions of others, they can drive social and ecological transformations. Lifestyle changes such as taking shorter showers and fewer car and plane trips, turning down heating or eating more plant-based meals all add up to significant carbon reductions when undertaken by millions of people. A recent report identifies thirty behavioural solutions that individuals could adopt which would lessen global emissions from anywhere between 20% and 37%, if scaled up across communities and countries through collective action.[3] Much more action than this is needed of course. Nevertheless, it is a helpful contribution which stimulates cultural change by demonstrating the viability and cumulative effect of daily actions in response to the climate crisis.

Developing a systemic worldview that links individual behaviours to collective action can ease burdens of feeling individually responsible for saving the planet every time we go to the shops. At the same time it cultivates hope and empowerment every time we do make choices that consciously connect individual actions to systemic processes. Collective actions such as joining a boycott of furniture made from rainforest trees, or making a shift to a superannuation scheme that does not invest in fossil fuels are shifting business practices through their cumulative effects. The refusal to consume destructive products and lifestyles makes them less profitable, while establishing new social norms. Co-ordinated consumer environmental action reshapes peoples' identities as global citizens who actively care for our planetary home, while often helping to reshape business and governmental practices.

One woman who recognises the creative coupling of individual empowerment with collective action is Natalie Isaacs, the founder of the Australian climate activist group 1 Million Women. For twenty-four years, Isaacs was a cosmetic manufacturer who knew about climate change but thought it was someone else's problem. She remembers:

> I could sit around a dinner table and talk about the issues and understand the dire consequences if we don't all act, then leave the dinner table and carry on business as usual.[4]

Isaacs also remembers shying away from the topic because she didn't want to feel silly in front of others because she didn't know enough or how to begin to respond. But in 2007 she had an epiphany, following watching Al Gore's *Inconvenient Truth*, and a brutal early spring bush fire season. An even stronger catalyst was reducing her electricity consumption by 20% and seeing the result on her bill, and then reducing her household food waste by 80%. For her, seeing what she could achieve was the point of emotional connection and taking ownership of the climate issue:

> *I realised every single thing we do shapes the kind of world we want to live in. I realised that as individuals and as a collective we are incredibly powerful* [italics added]. That's what led me to start 1 Million Women (1MW) a few years later.[5]

Today 1 Million Women is a global movement of 500,000 members, which campaigns to raise climate crisis awareness, lower carbon emissions, cut waste and advocate for effective climate policies. Its mission is grounded in the view that "one small action at a time multiplied by millions and millions changes the system." The inspiration and practicality of their daily social media posts empower followers to adopt ecologically mindful behaviours and to champion climate justice issues.

The climate crisis is proving to be the catalyst for many epiphanies that make the connection between daily life, social action and global ecosystems. In this chapter there are many stories about the intertwining of changing consciousness and changing behaviours in response to climate disruption. Experience shows that sometimes a change of understanding leads to behavioural change, and sometimes it is vice versa. It takes time, practice and social support to transform beginning initiatives into deep-seated change. Research psychologist Thupten Jinpa describes the ways that the brain changes in response to new experiences and interactions, noting how:

> through repetition over time, we come to internalize and embody a certain way of seeing, feeling and being in the world. Even tasks that initially require deliberate conscious effort can eventually become effortless and spontaneous.[6]

When we embody and internalise decisions we make in response to ecological destructions, we turn intention and information into a new way of being and living. Right now, all over the world millions, if not billions, of people are in the process of doing just this to a smaller or larger extent in their daily lives. This process not only feeds into cultural change, it also rewires minds. Each committed action to care for our planet, no matter how small it may seem, develops consciousness about who we are and how to live well in an ecological world.

Challenging consumerism

When I first started my research, one of the things I wanted to find out was at what stage I would positively embrace ecologically conscious changes in my lifestyle, rather than undertake them in a will-driven way because I felt I should. I knew if I could not do this, any changes of behaviour I attempted would be short-lived, and that I would have failed to live the change I wanted to see in others. I hoped that I would be able to find a way to reach this transformative place where ecological consciousness was integrated into my way of being, but I really did not know if it was possible. Nor was I sure how desirable or valuable it was to do this. But I did know that I wanted to give it a try, as well as learn from others who were on the same track as me but further along.

Speaking from personal experience and as a psychotherapist, I know consciousness change is neither speedy nor smooth. It typically generates conflict within ourselves, as well as with others we are close to who may prefer the predictable "old" consciousness to this disruptive "new" one. In the process of deep change, we can go back and forward, trying out new behaviours while experiencing a backwash of resistance, within ourselves and from others. Confusion often prevails as neither the old nor the new consciousness feels certain or secure. Having a safe place to explore all of this with like-minded others makes a world of difference.

The research group I facilitated provided just such a safe space with its ongoing discussions about the ins and outs, and ups and downs of our thoughts and actions in response to climate disruption. It turned fraught topics into fascinating, and frequently funny, ones. To my delight, by the end of the year it both increased my commitment to lower my emissions, and my pleasure in doing so. Some of this was due to peer encouragement, but some of it was also because it was liberating and intriguing to have honest discussions about conflicted emotions and experiences. There were many laughs about becoming "too hairshirty," as we called it, and many reflections about what it means and feels like to live within an emergent systemic worldview. We shared feelings of grief, shame, guilt, frustration, ignorance and isolation as we worked out ways of living that felt consistent with what we knew about the world and the practicalities of our life's circumstances. And we talked about how often we failed within the nitty gritty pressures of daily life. It was an honest process that generated empathy for ourselves and for others, as we became conscious of just how provocative this territory could be. Beneath the questions about what we could and should do to reduce our carbon emissions, lurked confronting questions about who we were and what mattered most to us.

One powerful change that occurred for me during this period began with a shocking dream which I had the night before my husband and I travelled overseas to attend a series of conferences. I had conflicting emotions about this trip. While I was very excited about this trip, I also felt guilty about the high greenhouse gas emissions involved in flying long distance. In this dream I witnessed people having the skin on their arms removed and replaced with grafts of hairless skin. Some people, including my neighbours, were also laying polished floorboards in their garages. Interspersed with these scenes were highly disturbing images of monkeys being slaughtered, and thrown on the jungle ground with their brains bashed out. In the dream I knew this monkey slaughter was a consequence of people's choices to have skin grafts and polished garage floorboards. I thought "No way, I'm never doing this" but I knew that more than just this personal refusal to participate in wasteful fashionable consumer behaviours was needed to address these shocking scenes.

My dream's shocking images stayed with me throughout our travels and their impact became magnified when my suitcase was lost in transit on the first leg of our trip. My baggage never turned up which meant that for six weeks I travelled questioning which of my lost possessions I really needed to replace along with the true costs of anything that I did consider buying. Old assumptions about needing to look good when presenting at conferences and meeting new people were challenged by my emerging awareness of the ecological costs of every purchase, providing a major impetus for transforming my shopping habits. Over and over again I asked what were my real needs, and what else could I do in response to my dream besides not buying stuff to "look good." On my return home, sharing this dream with the research group helped me to explore other layers of meanings and responses. Everyone could relate to the dream in some way or other, so that its images and themes recurred through subsequent group conversations. It turned out that my dream was the best possible luggage for the trip, offering learning which went way beyond any conference presentation.

We often need to be shocked or jolted out of familiar thoughts and behaviours in order to develop. Dreams offer this possibility. Jung wrote that when we run into an impasse in life, dreams can show us "the unvarnished, natural truth," returning consciousness to its foundations, while delivering insights that transform attitudes that led to the impasse.[7] The unvarnished truths of my dream about the murderous costs of consumer aspirations and lifestyles worked far more deeply into my psyche than could any listing of statistics about species loss or rainforest destructions.

My patterns of consumption substantially reduced after this dream. I understood the massacre literally, in relationship to rainforest destructions for logging and palm oil. And I also understood it at a psychological level, where it symbolised the many ways that the culture I live in denies human embeddedness in the animal world, banishing hairy skin and covering over the dirt that we live upon and that sustains us. Since then, without any great effort, a lot of stuff has lost its appeal. My desire to dress up myself or my home to "look good" has waned hugely. And when I do shop for anything other than food or plants (my particular weakness), the charity shop is my first port of call. At the same time I keep questioning what is the "more that is needed"? On a personal level, the dream helped me to challenge self-centred desires, and to become more committed to caring for the natural world. At a social level, the need to be involved in collective actions and responses to the climate crisis has become a very high priority.

In order to move beyond the insidious influences of hyper-consumer culture, we do need to find ways of hearing and talking about its hidden destructive dimensions. The symbolic language of dreams, images and stories can play a vital part in challenging deceptive images and undermining narratives of a fragile consumer identity. Symbol, metaphor and stories are a tremendous boon in facilitating consciousness change because they cut through intellectual defences. Their ability to speak on many levels at once can open us up to the difficult knowledge that we can all be perpetrators of violent destructions in the course of "normal life." By offering new visions and mobilising different forms of response, they help to forge connections to habitual places of disconnection, something I explore further in the last chapter of this book. Symbolic language and narratives can also be used manipulatively. A great deal of psychological research goes into the ways that advertising messages can influence people at conscious and unconscious levels. Advertising is designed to change our minds, our moods, our self-image and our behaviours. To protect ourselves from the incessant advertising present in consumerist cultures we need to identify and interrogate its use of symbolic images and subliminal messaging. Advertising under capitalism cultivates social values of competitiveness, individualism and entitlement. It links human desires for status, freedom, choice, purity and excitement to the purchase of stuff. When we succumb to its influences, it enlivens what Buddhists call the *hungry ghosts* in us, who are always on the lookout for something to feed our inner feelings of insecurity and emptiness.

Psychoanalyst Sally Weintrobe describes how the consumerist worldview operates as a colonising force invading our minds from an early age, repressing an authentic sense of self and a realistic view of life.[8] This worldview not only oils capitalist economic systems based on destructive models of endless growth and consumption, it also encourages us to see "ourselves as special, and as entitled, not only to our possessions, but to our 'quick fixes' to the problems of reality."[9] When gripped by this quick fix mentality, it is easy to think that climate change is not so bad or to assume that it will be magically solved by some smart new technology. This kind of thinking reinforces the status quo by avoiding the reality of climate destructions and the urgent need to respond appropriately through radical personal, social and political change. Furthermore, as ecopsychologist Mary Jayne Rust points out, the promotion and accessibility of quick fix solutions makes it harder for people to develop the capacity to tolerate short-term frustrations for the benefit of long-term satisfactions and outcomes.[10]

Rosemary Randall is a psychotherapist who understands the psychological processes that accompany radical change in response to climate disruption. She is the co-founder, with Andy Brown, of the highly successful Carbon Conversations programme which brings together small groups of people to work towards their intention of halving their individual carbon footprints.[11] Randall and Brown believe that people who want to respond constructively to the climate crisis need help in understanding and working through complex reactions to it in a supportive milieu. In Carbon Conversation groups, participants are encouraged to discuss the emotional impacts of climate change and their individual efforts to address it. This helps people to air the conflicts, regrets, fears and sadness provoked by changing lifestyles and consumption patterns, as well as to share the discoveries, satisfactions and liberations that are also part of this process.

Randall observes that contemporary affluent cultures, with all of their flexibilities and choices lack solid reference points. People shift home and jobs much more frequently than in the past and religious affiliations are on the decline. Identity, writes Randall, has "become a personal project of self ... something that is shopped for, supported by lifestyle choices and purchases."[12] This consumer identity is fragile and transient, lacking secure grounding in the natural world, or interior experience. Buying stuff acts as a compensation for a lack of internal substance, an attempt to define self, status and feelings of belonging.

When possessions are linked to our deepest desires and aspirations, they become wired into our identities. For many people even the thought of relinquishing desired and prized possessions can provoke significant feelings of loss of self. To deny ourselves "stuff" can trigger feelings of loss of identity, loss of freedom, loss of choice and loss of excitement; a deeply unappealing prospect, which the advertising industry uses manipulatively. For this reason, collective and peer support is vital to help people negotiate their way out of this consumer trap. In Carbon Conversation groups, participants can reflect on what their possessions and lifestyles mean to them, and what difference it makes to know the carbon costs of them. Randall believes that being able to grieve the losses of reduced consumption with others is vital in making a positive transition to a carbon conscious lifestyle. Without this recognition of the sadness of loss, she observes that resistance, resentment and bitterness can readily arise in response to the pressure to lower emissions.[13]

In a world of rapidly escalating climate disruption, the impetus for consciousness change can be strong, sudden and often shocking. To respond well to this impetus, we need to join with others to learn about the destructions, understand the turmoil this brings and figure out the best ways to respond. When people not only understand, but also feel the ecological and psychological costs of consumerism, they can cultivate forms of care and self-worth that do not revolve around consumerism or other quick fixes. This takes time and perseverance, as well as support from community groups such as Carbon Conversations or 1 Million Women.

I believe freeing the mind from unconscious consumerist imperatives is an evolutionary and a revolutionary act. Making a personal connection between the climate crisis and the thrall of consumer culture, is confronting but also liberating. The more we can reflect on our underlying discomforting feelings, such as desire, guilt, grief, fear, ambivalence, vulnerability and confusion, the more we develop the psychological maturity to counter the narcissistic drives promoted by consumer cultures. We can also find genuine delight, suggests Mary Jayne Rust, through asking ourselves the question "what is it we are really hungry for?"[14] Making this process a collective discussion cultivates mindful living attuned to the complexity and depth of ourselves and our world.

Motivating emotions

Acknowledging climate disruption can stir up a lot of guilt, especially if you live in a high emissions society. The more you learn about carbon emitting activities, the more the potential for guilt about daily activities such as travel and shopping. Many people distance themselves from climate concerns because they do not know how to respond to these feelings of guilt. Guilt is a fraught and difficult yet necessary emotion for human development. In its most functional capacity, guilt facilitates an examination of actions and conscience, the development of personal responsibility and a moral code for just and healing responses. But when it becomes dysfunctional, guilt overwhelms and incapacitates with negative judgements about oneself and one's ability to ever make good on a wrong. When it comes to climate guilt, there is a fine line to be trod between what is functional and what is dysfunctional.

A modicum of climate guilt, understood within the context of a systemic view, can be a catalyst for questioning ego-centric attitudes that ride high on feelings of personal entitlement, much encouraged within consumer societies. It may also be a first step towards healing a sense of separation from our natural world and embracing ecological values and worldviews. The guilt I felt in response to the dream I described in the previous section of this chapter certainly had this effect on me. However, guilt, like fear is a double-edged sword when it comes to motivating climate action. While some timely guilt does have its psychological uses for reassessing habitual assumptions and behaviours, it is not an effective foundation for long-term change. Campaigns that overdo the personal guilt message tend to backfire, either provoking defensive reactions of denial or overwhelming feelings of hopelessness.[15] And if guilt becomes a chronic pattern of response it can have depressive and paralysing effects, which contribute to a lowering of self-esteem and to feelings of disempowerment.

In her research into the concept of ecological debt, Rosemary Randall found that some people who had taken significant action to reduce their carbon footprints still struggled with feelings of guilt. One problem, she points out is that "it is difficult to make reparation if no one sees and accepts your gift."[16] However, actions that "were intrinsically creative and had benefit to others" felt more significant, especially when connected to healing our natural world, such as tree planting initiatives.[17] It also helped when people could maintain a sense of proportionality by understanding the larger political dimensions of the problem, so they felt less personally at fault.

The psychological effects of climate guilt are particularly harsh on individuals living within social and political domains that are in denial. When governments and corporations refuse to act responsibly by committing to sharp reductions of greenhouse gases, ecologically aware people can overcompensate by taking on far more than their fair share of responsibility for the causes and effects of climate upheaval. As a result, sensitive and caring individuals may end up feeling overloaded with feelings of personal and collective guilt. Which is neither a fair outcome, nor a good recipe for personal change or for influencing others. However, this does not mean that climate guilt should be denied or avoided, but that it needs to be experienced, understood and shared collectively within a social and political context, so it can become less of a source of misery and more of an impetus for care and repair.

Research shows that the best motivators for pro-environmental behaviour change are emotional appeals, social incentives,[18] and a renewal of connection to the natural world.[19] A campaign to increase adoption of cleaner, more efficient cookstoves in China's Yunnan province provides one example:

> A core activity in the campaign was a cooking contest among teams of women in the community to make the best versions of three local dishes using the efficient cook stoves. This contest not only helped the women familiarize themselves with the new

stoves, but it also gave them a chance to feel mastery and pride in a valued skill while having fun and working towards the betterment of their community.[20]

Other activities running along with the competition included a puppet show, traditional dancing and the adoption of the Hoolock gibbon, a local endangered species, as a mascot for the community. This campaign initiated by Rare, an organisation promoting behavioural change for conservation, succeeded in increasing the adoption of clean cookstoves from 18% to 59%. As a result, the forest habitat of the Hoolock gibbon improved as demand for wood for ovens decreased. Creative campaigns like this work because they generate positive emotions, increase connection to our natural world and empower individual action within collective contexts and frameworks. They not only encourage action, they also bond people to others and the world, contributing to an embodied experience of being part of ecosystems.

People need to feel good in their engagement. Joy, pride and increased relatedness to others and the natural world maximise people's commitment to the behavioural and social change required by climate disruption. This does not mean that there is no place for feelings of grief, guilt and fear to be felt and acknowledged within climate campaigns. They are all part of the emotional process of engaging with ecological destructions. But for us to bring the best of our creative efforts to the collective table we also need to cultivate enjoyment and connections that generate and sustain ongoing behavioural and social change.

Waking up to waste

One important trigger for cultural change is the disruption of silences and taboos. Acknowledgement of waste and its ecological consequences has been a source of major denial in industrialised societies. Waste is referred to as rubbish or garbage, reflecting a non-ecological worldview that believes waste has no function or consequences. It is just the unwanted, accidental stuff that is thrown away, or pumped into the atmosphere. But an ecological worldview reveals that there is no such place as "away" where waste can go. Whatever humans discard stays here, in one form or another, with complex ecological consequences.

All cultural worldviews make distinctions about what is clean and safe, and what is dirty and dangerous. Western-orientated cultures, estranged from the world's natural processes, have held negative judgements about any earthy waste. Rather than seeing waste as an inevitable and vital aspect of life on our planet, it is frequently perceived as shameful, distasteful, a failure or a boring inconvenience. These moralising views towards waste, combined with dismissive attitudes, breed resistance to, and resentment about, having to deal with it. They also fuel denials about its actual existence, as is evident in climate debates. When all waste is viewed as dirty, undesirable, or even non-existent, no distinction is made between functional waste, which can be safely transformed into something of value, and dysfunctional waste which poses threats to humans and other forms of life.

Engagement with the consequences of toxic wastes produced by developing and techno-industrialised nations dismantles modernist cultural assumptions and taboos. While consumer culture promises shiny germfree surfaces and bright new identities, it results in overflowing rubbish tips, resistant bacteria and rising temperatures. What consumerism renders invisible is fast gaining visibility. Wherever we go these days there is human produced waste; plastics in the oceans and on mountain tops, overflowing landfills and toxic chemicals in rivers and farmlands. The effects of increasing greenhouse gases in the atmosphere are also more visible. Talk about the weather has transformed from light chitchat to a confrontation with the global effects of human waste.

It takes cultural education, debate and leadership to develop a positive and open approach to what has been censored and avoided. Over the last one hundred years, the cultural work of transforming strongly-held taboos about sex into more enlightened discussions, behaviours and mores has been a strong feature of social transformation in many parts of the world. A similar wave of cultural change is now doing the work of transforming waste from an "unmentionable" into something necessary and even desirable to discuss. Waste products are starting to become fashionable as the potentials of recycling and repurposing transform "waste work" from a shameful occupation into a creative and meaningful practice. Rather than turn a blind eye and run, many people are demonstrating how engaging with waste issues can be a catalyst for a change of life and consciousness.

Bea Johnson, a Frenchwoman who lives in California, is one such person. Johnson is a pioneer of the Zero waste movement with its mantra of the 5Rs: Refuse, Reduce, Reuse, Recycle and Rot. It all began in 2006 when she and her family downsized from a suburban home to a rental apartment. This experience revealed to her that:

> when you live with less, you have more time to do what is important to you ... hikes, spending time with family, and doing picnics.[21]
>
> ... It's a life based on experiences instead of things and once you have that vision ... you can't go back. Because you fully see the old life as a waste of time and money ... based on the wrong priorities.[22]

As well as downsizing her possessions, Johnson and her husband embarked upon a process of education about the environmental impacts of waste which "really made us sad" and provoked fears about their children's future.[23] As a result, Johnson radically reduced her household waste and set up a blog promoting zero waste solutions. While Johnson's husband was sceptical that their changing household habits would make a difference in the world, he was proved wrong.[24] Typically, Johnson's website gets over two hundred and fifty thousand views a month, and each week an email arrives from someone who has been inspired to open a low waste bulk food store.

The zero waste movement shows the power of linking individual to collective responses and working from the ground up on a wide range of issues including bans on single use plastics and the adoption of "cradle to cradle" manufacturing. Just as importantly, it is succeeding in breaking old cultural taboos and silences by making waste a repeated topic of discussion across the dinner table, in boardrooms and in Parliaments. When we talk about dealing with waste we need to acknowledge the discomforts this can stir up, as well as the need to do things differently. Overflowing rubbish dumps reveal the transience of stuff and the inevitability of our own "wasting away." The local tip is rich in possibilities for thoughts about mortality and legacy. Material waste and greenhouse gas emissions also confront us with the wastefulness of contemporary lifestyles, readily stirring up feelings of shame and guilt. We need to talk about these kinds of emotional responses to counteract collective taboos and denials about waste.

Just as some people might feel overwhelmed by collective guilt in the absence of responsible climate action, others can feel overwhelmed by collective shame within a society that refuses to "deal with its own shit." If anything, ecological shame can be even more paralysing than ecological guilt, as it stirs up a primitive urge to hide (or hide from) the source of the shame. Desires and fantasies to live in perfect cleanliness or visit pristine places can be an unconscious attempt to escape shame about waste.

The pursuit of ecological purity arises from an unconscious attempt to disentangle ourselves from the destructive elements of being human. The attempt to maintain a position of personal purity can lead to projecting all responsibility for destructiveness on to other people or groups (such as Donald Trump or fossil fuel companies). The development of ecological consciousness reveals the ways that everyone in techno-industrialised societies is implicated to some degree or another in contributing to ecological destructions. This understanding by no means absolves governments or corporate powers from responsibility for their hugely destructive actions and denials, but it does help to counter polarising judgements. When we recognise the mutuality of our predicament, it opens the way to engaging with the complexity of our shared destructions. Learning to identify our own shame about waste, rather than avoiding it, encourages actions we can all undertake.

Accepting that we are all messy and destructive at times frees the mind and imagination to tackle waste creatively. These days, social media is full of intriguing waste solutions from edible plates to roads built out of recycled plastic. Finding new ways, and recovering old ways, to recognise, reduce, reuse and recycle waste is an experimental journey, which can be as exciting and uncertain as the world is. Even with the best intentions, there are always unintended effects. In this situation, we need to not let "the perfect" be the enemy of "the better."

As I write, there is a recycling crisis in industrialised nations who have relied on China to do the hard work of their plastic recycling. But now China has closed its doors to dealing with the plastic waste of other nations. So each time I put my recycling bin out for collection, I know the plastic is probably being stockpiled with a good chance of ending up in landfill. What good feelings I had about plastic waste collection for recycling have evaporated. Now, I am attempting to shop more in bulk stores and boycott products in plastic containers. As I do so, I am encountering all the usual mixed feelings and mixed results of early behavioural change. At the same time, I am making more effort to sign petitions and write letters to businesses and governments to accept responsibility for reducing and recycling plastic. Dealing with waste is work in progress, requiring constant feedback and assessment. It is a rich teacher about the basics of earthy life and the ways that our lives, and indeed ourselves, are all woven into the ongoing cycles of creation, destruction, transformation and evolution on Earth.

Climate crisis drives home the reality that in a systemic world the consequences of any action can never be fully known. It is vital to acknowledge and discuss the confusions and failures of our individual and collective attempts to establish sustainable behaviours, as well as the successes. Acknowledging that there are no perfect solutions provides a reality check and reduces anxiety. It also helps to develop a more conscious understanding of eco-systemic complexity and our place within it. We are not gods ordering the world, but messy participants, learning as we go.

In the company of others

At an individual level, a less than perfect green lifestyle will not single-handedly destroy the planet. However, understood at a collective level, our personal actions might contribute to inflicting significant ecological damage, just as they might play a part in supporting the healings of ecosystems and establishing ecologically aware social norms. Learning to approach daily life as an opportunity to enact ecological values is empowering for yourself and inspiring for others. Especially if you can open up conversations about this with others in empathic and non-judgemental ways.

Research from the fields of social and environmental psychology demonstrates the crucial influence of peer behaviour, beliefs and values. In their review of the role of social psychology's contribution to addressing environmental problems, Susan Koger and Deborah Winter conclude "If there is any single message from social psychology, it is that changes are much easier to make and keep if we put ourselves in social situations that support them."[25] Personal change occurs in relation to others. Sometimes we change because of one influential person or peer group, sometimes as a result of a social movement reaching a critical mass which normalises new thinking and actions. This social factor of change is vitally important in the transition to low carbon societies.

My friend Lisa Roberts, the founder of Living Data, a social and digital network that brings together understandings from art and science, tells the story of making the transition to a low-emissions lifestyle through meeting her partner some twenty years ago. When she started living with her partner, he had already worked out how to lessen his carbon footprint. Lisa remembers that this was a great boon for her because although she wanted to live in a low ecological impact way she didn't know how to do this. She says:

> I hate making decisions. I can't calculate by going down the shopping aisles and looking at all the labels. He does all that, so I have learnt … it's easy for me … I was thinking that way, and here he was doing it.

While her partner's leadership and expertise opened the way for change, Lisa still had to negotiate her own and others' judgements. Peer expectation can act in a number of ways after all. Lisa observes:

> People feel sorry for me because [of how] I live … We go out for dinner, and it's fish and chips: that's our big night … we don't go to restaurants … and I used to flinch at that; I thought "I'm not loved, he's not spending money on me."

A change of behaviour based on ecological consciousness is also a change of beliefs and a change of meanings. Lisa had to work through her own anxiety about how much she was loved, when she realised there would be no fancy restaurant dates in her relationship. But over time, this carbon conscious way of living has "just become a way of living" for Lisa – one that aligns with her values, and inspires her development of a wide range of ecologically based creative projects, enthusiastically supported by her partner.

In order to shift to low carbon lifestyles, we need leadership, companionship and open discussions. Breaking established norms, personal and social, stirs up discomforting feelings, usually related to our own or other's judgements. Noticing and negotiating condemnations, internal or external, is challenging. Conditioning, ignorance, fear, guilt, grief, shame and competitiveness inform judgemental responses. This can be confronting to recognise. But it also can be enlivening when it spurs questions about the origin and nature of the judgements we encounter in ourselves and others. As so many psychotherapists observe, we most often condemn in others what we repress in ourselves. It is only when we explore this in ourselves and with others that we can then find the insight to liberate ourselves from being driven by judgements that are a poor fit with the realities of life and the core values that matter most to us.

Engaging with today's ecological crises ramps up the possibilities and scope of self-realisation. Climate crisis in particular supercharges perennial existential questions about who we are, what really matters, and the nature of life. Even a trip to the shops can expand consciousness at an individual and universal level when we surrender to soul-searching questions such as: What do I really need? What do I have an appetite for? What are the true costs and benefits? What are the pressures? What are the consequences of my decisions for others, human and other than human? How do my choices reflect the fullness of my being? Walking the supermarket aisles can be as much of a consciousness-raising exercise as any spiritual retreat. Both pose questions and opportunities for recognising the effects of social conditioning, the consequences of being driven by unexamined desires and judgements, the fluidity of self-identity, the inter-relationship of all beings and the guiding momentum of values.

Sharing values

Tensions and conflicts are inevitable when reassessing life meanings and values in a climate disrupted world. Many social scientists (following the work of sociologist Shalom Schwartz) describe people as having a mix of *self-enhancement* values, which support the pursuit of personal and social success through individual prosperity and power, and *self-transcendence* values, which support the appreciation, care and protection of others and nature.[26] Recent generations have been socially conditioned into a bias towards self-enhancement values through the status-seeking appeals of commercial advertising, celebrity culture, consumerist patterning, social media platforms and governmental policies which prioritise economic concerns over participation in community life and care for the environment. As Naomi Klein describes it, "denigration of collective action and veneration of the profit motive have infiltrated virtually every government on the planet, every major media organisation, every university, our very souls."[27] To address the many catastrophic consequences of this values bias, we need to collectively and individually reflect and engage with self-transcendent values of connection and concern for the welfare of all.

The work of countering neoliberal social biases towards self-enhancement values begins with the recognition that there is a dynamic tension between both sets of values in each of us. To some extent, we all look out for ourselves and care about others. Acknowledging our internal conflicts around values spurs individuation as it deepens self-knowledge and empathy for others. Without this acknowledgement, it is easy to project what we do not recognise in ourselves onto others. This fuels polarising attitudes and blanket condemnations which can turn people into enemies and stereotypes, like the "heartless mining lobbyist" or the "bleeding heart Greenie." When we learn to identify and negotiate the mix of values in ourselves and others, it can stimulate fruitful dialogues about shared and shifting values, and their consequences.

Cultivating an awareness about social values is vital when communicating about climate disruption. For example, climate communications that employ guilt-tripping messages threaten people's self-enhancing values. Tom Crompton, co-founder of the Common Cause Foundation, notes that climate campaigns based upon self-enhancement values, such as promoting carbon reductions in order to save money, or buying green products to boost social status, tend to be ineffective as they reinforce the values behind the problem instead of offering an alternative set of values.[28] The most effective environmental campaigns appeal to the self-transcendent values that encourage empathy, care and feelings of belonging.

Research by the Common Cause Foundation in the United Kingdom shows that the majority of people (74%) have compassionate (self-transcendent) values.[29] However, most people (77%) underestimate how much their fellow citizens do care about others and the world, which is problematic because it acts as a disincentive for community involvement. The most likely reason for this underestimation is the amount of air space given to selfish (self-enhancement) values by public institutions and the media. One antidote to this destructive cultural bias is to encourage more people to talk in public spaces about what matters most to them. Crompton's campaigning work focuses on promoting conversations between people about what truly matters. Common Cause's research found that:

> people who hold truer perspectives of others' values report deeper connection to their communities, show greater motivation to become civically engaged, are more likely to support action on social or environmental challenges, and have higher wellbeing.[30]

Healthy societies need respectful, open and in-depth public conversations. To care for our world we need to listen and talk with others more often about what matters most. Then we can find out just how much we all have in common.

Community projects that encourage people to think and talk about what really matters in life are essential for climate action. While many fear that humanity cannot be trusted to respond to climate-driven catastrophes, disasters can be a time when the self-transcendent values of care, kindness and communality come to the fore in the majority of people, as Rebecca Solnit describes in her book *A Paradise Built in Hell*.[31] In times of emergency we tend to remember what really matters, that we depend on each other, and that our deepest wellbeing and happiness lies in community. One benefit of talking about the climate crisis as an emergency is that it provides an opening to communicate more about collaborative efforts and re-ordering community values in response to disaster.[32]

To address the present and pending disasters of climate crisis, we need to hear more personal stories not just the statistics. We also need to enter into conversations, with ourselves, our loved ones, our colleagues and our communities about what really matters and how this might be embedded in our daily lives. Such conversations revitalise people and re-energise schools, universities, workplaces, faith-based communities and cultural institutions to develop caring initiatives and boost self-transcendent values. In the next chapter we hear how the climate crisis is spurring collective conversations and actions that foster ecological healing and cultural change.

Notes

1 Weintrobe, S. (2015, Dec 2). A new imagination. Retrieved from www.climatepsychologyalliance.org/explorations/papers/103-anew-imagination
2 Bright, B. & Marshall, J. (2019). Jonathan Marshall interviewed by Bonnie Bright. *Earth Climate Dreams*.
3 Williamson, K., Satre-Meloy, A., Velasco, K. & Green, K. (2018). Climate change needs behavior change: Making the case for behavioral solutions to reduce global warming. Arlington, VA: Rare.
4 Isaacs, N. (2017, Mar 9). My personal journey on becoming an empowered woman. Retrieved from www.1millionwomen.com.au/blog/my-personal-journey-becoming-empowered-woman/
5 www.1millionwomen.com.au/our-movement/about-1-million-women/
6 Jinpa, T. (2015). *A fearless heart: Why compassion is the key to greater wellbeing*. London, UK: Piatkus, pp. 233–234.

7 Jung, C. G. (1964). *Civilisation in transition.* (CW, Vol. 10). London, UK: Routledge & Kegan Paul, p. 149.
8 Weintrobe, S. (2013). Love of nature and human nature. In S. Weintrobe (Ed.), *Engaging with climate change: Psychoanalytic and interdisciplinary perspectives.* Hove, UK: Routledge, p. 203.
9 Weintrobe, S. (2013). The difficult problem of anxiety in thinking about climate change. In S. Weintrobe (Ed.), *Engaging with climate change: Psychoanalytic and interdisciplinary perspectives.* Hove, UK: Routledge, p. 43.
10 Rust, M-J. (2012). Ecological intimacy. In M.-J. Rust & N. Totton (Eds.), *Vital signs: Psychological responses to ecological crisis.* London, UK: Karnac, p. 156.
11 www.carbonconversations.co.uk/
12 Randall, R. (2012). Fragile identities and consumption: The use of "Carbon Conversations" in changing people's relationship to "stuff". In M.-J. Rust & N. Totton (Eds.), *Vital Signs: Psychological responses to ecological crisis.* London, UK: Karnac, p. 227.
13 Ibid.
14 Rust, M-J. (2012). Ecological intimacy. In M.-J. Rust & N. Totton (Eds.), *Vital signs: Psychological responses to ecological crisis.* London, UK: Karnac, p. 157.
15 Schneider, C. R., Zaval, L., Weber, E. U. & Markowitz, E. M. (2017). The influence of anticipated pride and guilt on pro-environmental decision making. *PLOS ONE 12* (11). Retrieved from https://doi.org/10.1371/journal.pone.0188781
16 Randall, R. (2013). Great expectations: The psychodynamics of ecological debt. In S. Weintrobe (Ed.), *Engaging with climate change: Psychoanalytic and interdisciplinary perspectives.* Hove, UK: Routledge, p. 94.
17 Ibid, pp. 94–95.
18 Williamson, K., Satre-Meloy, A., Velasco, K. & Green, K. (2018). *Climate change needs behavior change: Making the case for behavioral solutions to reduce global warming.* Arlington, VA: Rare. Retrieved from www.zestlabs.com/downloads/2018-CCNBC-Report.pdf
19 Amel, E., Manning, C., Scott, B. & Koger, S. (2017, Apr 20). Beyond the roots of human inaction: Fostering collective effort toward ecosystem conservation. *Science 356* (6335), 275–279.
20 Williamson, K., Satre-Meloy, A., Velasco, K. & Green, K. (2018). *Climate change needs behavior change: Making the case for behavioral solutions to reduce global warming.* Arlington, VA: Rare. Retrieved from www.zestlabs.com/downloads/2018-CCNBC-Report.pdf, p. 40.
21 Durbanova, A. (2017, Oct 20). Zero waste lifestyle: Interview with Bea Johnson. Retrieved from https://impakter.com/zero-waste-lifestyle-interview-bea-johnson/
22 You regret not starting earlier – you see your whole life as a waste of money and time. (2017, Mar 11). *The Journal.* Retrieved from www.thejournal.ie/article.php?id=3274554

23 Durbanova, A. (2017, Oct 20). Zero waste lifestyle: Interview with Bea Johnson. Retrieved from https://impakter.com/zero-waste-lifestyle-interview-bea-johnson/
24 Chang, C. (2017, Apr 29). What I learned from trying to live zero waste for a year. Retrieved from www.news.com.au/lifestyle/real-life/what-i-learned-from-trying-to-live-zero-waste-for-a-year/news-story/8ebfbe3355c9a218e2c7339e1a267472
25 Koger, S. M. & Winter, D. D. N. (2010). *The psychology of environmental problems: Psychology for sustainability* (3rd ed.). New York, NY: Psychology Press, p. 130.
26 Crompton, T. (2013). Discussion: On the love of nature and human nature. In S. Weintrobe (Ed.), *Engaging with climate change: Psychoanalytic and interdisciplinary perspectives*. Hove, UK: Karnac, pp. 221–225.
27 Klein, N. (2014). *This changes everything: Capitalism vs. climate*. New York, NY: Simon & Schuster, p. 62.
28 Crompton, T. (2013). Discussion: on the love of nature and human nature. In S. Weintrobe (Ed.), *Engaging with climate change: Psychoanalytic and interdisciplinary perspectives*. Hove, UK: Karnac, pp. 221–225.
29 The Common Cause UK values survey. Retrieved from https://valuesandframes.org/values-in-action/survey
30 Common Cause Foundation (2018–2019). Retrieved from https://valuesandframes.org/about-us.
31 Solnit, R. (2009). *A paradise built in hell: The extraordinary communities that arise in disaster*. New York, NY: Penguin.
32 Morton, J. (2019). *Don't mention the emergency?: Making the case for emergency climate action*. Melbourne, Australia: Darebin Climate Action Now.

Chapter 6

Sustaining action

Engaging with passion

"Yo! We're The Knitting Nannas, that's our name/Got to save it for the kiddies, that's our aim."[1] Activists come in all ages and colours. Some of the most surprising ones are the most effective. Like the Knitting Nannas Against Gas of the Northern Rivers region of New South Wales, who originally came together to oppose coal seam gas mining on their farms. Today there are more than forty *loops* (or groups) active in Australia, the United Kingdom and the United States. Decked out in their official colours of black and yellow, the Knitting Nannas conduct knitting sit ins, carry out cheeky stunts, offer support to younger protestors at blockades and even perform rap on YouTube. Behind their wisecracks, lies the steely grit of mature women committed "to peacefully protest against the destruction of our air, land and water by greedy people and greedy organisations."[2] For many it is their first taste of activism.

As co-founder Clare Twomey sees it, the Knitting Nannas are able to develop "an image far from the stereotype of feral protestors" while at the same time tackling "the problem of invisible older women [being] given stereotypical tasks, such as photocopying and tea making, in protest movements." Instead, the Nannas "knit up a revolution" with a spirit of levity which disarms police officers and defuses tensions at protests. They crochet yellow bikinis to adorn images of recalcitrant politicians and tie up mining rigs in knitted scarves. Some have been arrested and charged for taking part in non-violent actions. "After a certain age," says Clare "you don't care what people think of you."[3]

I first encountered the Knitting Nannas in their full glory at an anti-fracking demonstration on the streets of North Sydney, where corporations rule from armour-glassed skyscrapers. But on this particular morning, people power ruled at the doors of energy giant AGL as a festive rally celebrated the hundredth successive week of protests organised by a determined group of country folk from Gloucester, some two hundred kilometres north of here. The Knitting Nannas were guests of honour, ensconced in camp chairs, knitting hats and blankets in bumblebee colours. Anne Thompson stepped up to the microphone, looking like a cross between a fairy godmother and superwoman in her stylish black and yellow cape and hat. "I am seventy-five, a grandmother ... before I became a Knitting Nanna I had never slept in a tent" she tells us. But now she tells us she is having the time of her life, sleeping out at blockades, staging sit-ins and pursuing politicians with her Nanna companions, in order to protect precious farmlands and water tables.

For climate engagement to be sustainable, the depth and uniqueness of personal being needs to align with participation in social and systemic change. "Doing the right thing" is often draining and short lived, but finding a form of engagement that extends horizons and is full of heart and good humour energises and transforms lives. Writer and ecologist Thomas Berry offers wise words when he suggests "Maybe the answer is to fight always for what you particularly love, not abstractions."[4] Not everyone feels comfortable with the idea of becoming an activist, especially if their idea of activism is limited to attending rallies and carrying out direct action. While protests are vital in rallying support and exerting pressure for change, they are only one part of the landscape of climate engagement across the world. There is a huge range of possible responses and activities to address the climate emergency from neighbourhood initiatives like clothes swaps and car pools, through to community responses like urban farms and tree planting projects. And then there are national and international campaigns such as *Extinction Rebellion, 350.org* and *The Sum of Us* who work at political as well as economic levels through mass protests, shareholder actions and consumer boycotts.

So how do you want to respond to the climate crisis and the cultural change it necessitates?

There is virtually no passion, talent or circumstance that is irrelevant for caring for our world or transforming consciousness about the way we live. From yachties cleaning up floating islands of plastic, to barristers arguing for the legal rights for rivers, cultural change is happening through projects founded on inspiration and collaborative action, fed by the human desire for fulfilment, meaning and care for

Earth and the joy of making a difference. Effective climate action requires and builds sustained engagement, co-operative abilities and creative responses. Who we are, where we are, how we relate, and whatever we most love doing are all vital ingredients in the mix. What this recipe cooks up, as the Knitting Nannas demonstrate, is courageousness, curiosity, commitment, companionship and hopefully many laughs.

Nurturing resilience

Researching this book, I have read many stories about people transforming themselves and their lives through growing ecological consciousness. They are generally stories with many chapters and without an end. Like any change of consciousness, there is no going back to a life of not seeing, not knowing, or not responding. But there are many choices to be made, as well as phases of engagement to go through in the course of a lifetime. The climate crisis is going to be with us for a very long time. Engagement needs to be sustained, sustaining and sustainable.

Burnout is an ever-present danger for climate campaigners and scientists, not only because there is always more that is needing to be done, but also because for many people keeping constantly busy is an ingrained way to stave off feelings of despair, grief and anxiety. In societies where cultural conditioning rewards extroverted activity and discourages emotional expression or introspection, there is often little space or affirmation for self-reflection or consciousness change. Writing about activist burnout, Sophy Banks from the Transition Network observes how dynamics from mainstream culture inevitably show up in Transition groups because "it's part of our makeup – like the air we breathe." Observing an unhealthy balance between doing and being, Banks reflects on "my family's culture, where we talked about ideas and achievements, but never feelings; on the culture of Transition Network, which started with mostly action and very little reflection."[5]

Recognising cultural imbalances in our thinking and behaviour is a catalyst for consciousness change. Climate disruption is driven by economic models based upon assumptions about the necessity of endless growth of activity, productivity and consumption. These assumptions unconsciously work their way into people's psychological being and daily behaviours, creating conditions for burnout. If not challenged, speediness, overwork and heroic ambitions can be just as much a feature of climate action groups, as of board rooms, governments and universities. And they are more likely to inhibit transformational change than achieve it. To change the world, we need to change ourselves, often in ways that can be quite unexpected. The world does not require us to become martyrs to save the planet or ourselves. "Savour not saviour" is an effective mantra for balanced engagement with ecological issues. Finding a joyful way of being in our lives and world not only helps to keep connected with the challenges of our times, it is also a part of the solution. Buddhist teacher Pema Chödrön gives this reminder:

> Times are difficult globally; awakening is no longer a luxury or an ideal. We don't need to add more depression, more discouragement, or more anger to what is already here. It's becoming essential that we learn to relate sanely to difficult times. The earth seems to be beseeching us to connect with joy and discover our innermost essence.[6]

When we make the physical and emotional space to be with what delights and inspires us in the world, we resource ourselves for the challenges. And when we relish life and ourselves, we are not so susceptible to the external forces of market economies that pressure us into high patterns of consumption or high-speed lifestyles, so at odds with the needs of personal, social and ecological wellbeing.

Undoubtedly, one of the biggest challenges of being engaged with climate disruption is to be aware of its present and future dangers, without becoming overwhelmed by this knowledge. There is no one simple formula for how to do this, although ongoing self-care and peer support are truly vital. Some campaigners, like George Marshall, learn how "to keep that worry on one side; knowing that the threat is real, yet actively choosing not to feel it."[7] Many, however, find themselves on an emotional roller-coaster ride, especially in their early days of engagement. Psychiatrist Dr Lise Van Susteren, a graduate of Al Gore's *Inconvenient Truth* slide-show training, diagnoses climate distress as a form of *pre-traumatic* stress, noting how "So many of us are exhibiting all the signs and symptoms of posttraumatic disorder – the anger, the panic, the obsessive intrusive thoughts."[8] This distress is understandable but not helpful for healthy ongoing climate engagement. Climate work of any kind can only be sustainable when it is accompanied by self-care, nurturing social networks and, if needed, psychological support from professionals who are themselves aware of the climate emergency and the stresses and distresses this can trigger.

There can be a fine line between an unhealthy obsession and creative immersion, or disavowal and mindful detachment, when it comes to climate engagement. Clinician Leslie Davenport sums up this dilemma:

> We need real commitment to the climate movement in order to reverse our current destructive path, but rigid engagement can become obsessional and harden into an unintended obstacle. We need self-care, but when we seek balance it can be easy to slide into distancing and avoiding.[9]

Obviously, no one maintains any kind of perfect equilibrium here. After years of engagement, I still experience hours, days or even occasional weeks of overwhelm and despair, and at other times feelings of numbness and disconnection. Generally, the time span of my descents has shortened as I have learnt better how to recognise and respond to a lowering in my mood, most often associated with a fresh burst of unrecognised or untended grief. When I realise this is happening I allow myself to feel sad, to grieve, talk about what I am feeling with someone who can listen compassionately, and to write about it. I also know that I need to slow down, take time out and go somewhere or do something that I love.

In an account of her own climate activism burnout Gillian Caldwell recalls becoming "increasingly distraught" as she immersed herself in the science and early impacts of climate change.[10] But as a Campaign Director for the United States 1Sky campaign (which has since merged with 350.org) she "soldiered on" hoping that her busyness and sense of relief to be doing something about the crisis would stem her feelings of overwhelm. This strategy worked for a time but eventually she realised that she was "slipping." Recognising that she was not alone in this, Caldwell's response was to publicly speak with Lise van Susteren about her feelings of what she called "climate trauma."[11] She then went on to write an article about her experience, which included van Susteren's tips for climate trauma survival. These tips advocate a wide range of self-care practices along with advice to be realistic about what you can do, diversify activities so you are not always working on climate issues, maintain good boundaries between personal life and climate work and recognise how acknowledging and dealing with climate trauma builds resilience for sustained action.[12]

Learning to monitor and respond to moods and thoughts is vital for healthy climate engagement. For some activists, meditation or mindfulness practices provides a way to be with, and move through, distressing feelings aroused by climate issues. For others, creative expression and/or physical movement helps to contain shifting emotional states. For many, consciously connecting with the natural world, whether in the wilds, or in an urban park, is restorative. Swedish environmentalist Ann Murugan describes tackling her own feelings of despair and eco-anxiety by:

> cleaning up doom and gloom thoughts and beliefs in my head, and ... using mindfulness and mental training techniques. A practical example of one of the things that I did was to consciously shift my focus from previously spending about 95% of my time and energy on the problems, and 5% on the solutions, to instead start spending the majority of my time and energy on the solutions. As I did this, I started to feel less anxious and more hopeful. My connection to the Earth deepened. My energy increased and I felt environmentally inspired from a place of joy![13]

It can take a conscious commitment to not become mesmerised by the terrors and horrors of contemporary ecological destructions when you are well-informed about the climate emergency. As storyteller Martin Shaw succinctly observes, "If all you do is stare into hell, you will become ashes."[14] We need reflective, inspiring and joyful experiences in our activism, as well as time out from it.

In their research, Paul Hoggett and Rosemary Randall identified a number of key factors that enabled activists to maintain sustained engagement in a psychologically healthy way. These included excitement and pleasure in the actions themselves, social cohesion and support within the campaign group, community building within the campaigns and time out for self-care and reflection, including times spent in nature.[15] In other words, the way that campaigners worked and related to their peers and the natural world aligned with the values and joys that inspired their commitment and their visions for change. Being able to cultivate renewable resources in the form of understandings, relationships and activities that sustain and enthuse us for the long haul are a part of responding to the big picture. Just as climate disruption attunes attention to weather patterns in the world, so too can it heighten awareness of the sensitivities and fluctuations of personal wellbeing.

In his memoir *Oil and Honey*, writer and climate activist Bill McKibben explored the flux of external activity and internal states. He describes the ups and downs of becoming a climate campaign leader, alongside the story of his friendship and business partnership with Kirk Webster, a reclusive apiarist who teaches him about the life of bees and sustainable honey making. These "few blessed interludes in the beeyards" bring precious sustenance and inspiration.[16] McKibben writes of the pull between his commitment to campaign across the globe to keep coal and oil in the ground, and his "very nearly biological" need to stay close to home. For a while he was deeply bothered by how "the two sides of my life were so at odds" but over time he does find some kind of reconciliation between these two dimensions of himself and his life.[17] Not only because he and his beekeeper friend are able to support one and other from their differing places and experiences, but also because he can see that his "constant motion" and his beekeeper's friend "fixed gravity" are both anchored in their shared experiences of working with collective movements, one in the human world, the other in the insect world.

Meaning making, anchoring and balancing in life are all vital for sustained climate engagement. Being able to cultivate nourishing and inspiring resources in the form of understandings, relationships, skills, resting places and activities for the long haul is very much a part of responding to the big picture. A systemic view reveals how personal restoration can be interlinked with ecological reparation. Learning to slow down and rest up, as well as eating and exercising well, finding support, respecting limits and cultivating expanded perspectives of our world and ourselves, are all part of embodying ecological consciousness. We need to be grounded in natural processes to maintain engagement on the ground.

Hope as commitment

Over the last few years of writing this book, droughts, bushfires, heatwaves and cyclones have been intensifying, while climate action has been held back by right-wing governments. Like many others, I have been asking, "what kind of hope, if any, can I have as climate catastrophe escalates?" I am a natural optimist, so giving up hope for a good outcome of any situation is not easy for me. But in relation to climate, I have had to recognise when hope becomes a delusionary denial of deeply unwanted realities. Nevertheless, I do need some form of hope to feel like life is worth living and that there is meaning and purpose in my caring. These days the hope that gets me out of bed each morning is not the *everything will work out* kind of hope but one grounded in appreciation and love for life, whatever may come. I can have no idea what will happen for me, my loved ones, the next generations or our world's ecosystems, but I do know what matters and what I love, and I am able to act on this each day. There is hope in this.

Many others too are understanding hope as a commitment to action. For Joanna Macy, active hope is a practice that commits us to what we most deeply desire, rather than what we think may or may not be possible. When interviewed about his campaigning work for marine sanctuaries and coral reef protection, Tim Winton made the point that "Optimism isn't an emotion, it's an attitude, a discipline."[18] His view accords with Vaclev Havel's belief that "Hope is not a prognostication. It is an orientation of the spirit, an orientation of the heart," which works towards what is good, regardless of its chances of success.[19]

These perspectives move beyond intellect and pragmatism into the realms of philosophy and spirituality. They make hope an invitation for imaginative vision and soul making. It is a kind of hope which inspires us to make more of ourselves and our lives, while cherishing what is precious in our world. Hope in dark times requires ongoing nourishment as well as commitment and action. If my daily reading was only the news reports on climate disasters and failed climate action, I would not be writing this book, or engaging with the climate crisis on a daily basis. To keep acting and caring, I need a steady diet of what makes me love and care about this world: gardening, reading about nature, trips to the beach, yoga with girlfriends, dream group and dialogue circle meetings, the joy of my husband's company. Crucially important is to feel bonded with others through social movements committed to cultural and political change and ecological care, where my hope resides in what we can do together.

Authentic hope requires a gardener's patience to bear with fallow and fertile times, accepting risks and uncertainty, successes and failures. In a conference talk, psychoanalyst Sally Weintrobe observed that:

> Genuine hope, unlike false hope, is a trusted steadfast belief, strengthened by the part of us that cares, that we will find a way to face things truthfully, even when this brings difficult feelings and moral challenges, and even when we find ourselves stuck at times.[20]

The psychological work of maintaining hope involves mourning illusions and accepting reality. This work is ongoing and challenging. Weintrobe recounts an anecdote from her own life when a friend confronted her about the extent of her disappointment about other people's lack of climate action. His comment hit the mark. Weintrobe's anger and frustration gave way to feelings of despair and grief. She said:

> Facing my disappointment brought huge sadness. Was I mourning an illusion that people could change for the better, had my hopes for change been Pollyannaish, or was I simply more emotionally in touch with my feelings about our culture of uncare? I did not know. But with my anger having abated and given way to sadness and grieving my sense of hope began to resurface.[21]

Weintrobe's hope, after this experience, became more resolute. It strengthened "in a good and serviceable way" because she could grieve over a situation she did not want to be, but could now recognise and accept.

Genuine hope is not for the faint-hearted. It requires dreams and imagination to steer action towards what inspires and motivates us, and emotional stamina to keep faith through disappointments, failures and feelings of despair. The Climate Psychology Alliance believes that we need to cultivate *radical hope* in the face of the terrible reality of the climate crisis. Radical hope that works towards a new future through facing into present losses and grief. It requires a letting go of our old values and identifications, so that we can embrace what has been hidden in their shadow.[22] What this shadow might hold are suppressed emotions like despair, grief and rage, as well as assumptions of safety and entitlement. When we can acknowledge these kinds of habitual repressions and avoidances, it releases energy for experimentation, defiance and renewal.

Acts of defiance can be a means "to bring about some of what we hope for while we live by principle in the meantime," suggests Rebecca Solnit.[23] Michael Foster is a practitioner of this kind of defiant act. He is one of the five Valve Turners who, as "an act of moral necessity" briefly shut down the Keystone Pipeline one autumn morning in 2016. His engagement with climate issues has been a long and active one. He observes that:

Most of the people that I have met who are taking a consistent courageous part in the movement can talk to you about the moment when they lost hope, when they reached despair, and then they woke up the next day and said, "Okay, now what?" I think that despair is a critical ingredient for facing the existential emergency we inhabit. The tragedy overwhelms the mind's capacity to comprehend. Taking action is the only antidote, the only reason to hope.[24]

I don't believe that taking action is the only antidote or response we can have to despair, but it is a vital ingredient in cultivating the kind of hope that can maintain engagement with the dire circumstances of climate disruption. Equally important is accepting that feelings of despair will arise at times, as part of the ebb and flow of emotions that accompany major loss and change.

We need internal reflection and outer action, carried out in the company of others, to be able to bear with the existential threats of climate crisis. Learning to endure fluctuations of feelings including hope and despair, optimism and pessimism, confidence and doubt, expectation and disappointment builds emotional resilience and deep wisdom. When we can share how we feel with supportive others, it helps give context to our own and others' emotional oscillations. It is rare for everyone in a climate discussion to feel the same thing at the same time. As a collective, we can learn to witness and hold the range of shifting emotions of engagement, knowing that it is a swings and roundabouts process. Acknowledging and accepting see-sawing feelings or perspectives in ourselves and others activates a dynamic process that generates compassion, repair and renewal. Hope then becomes a compass of care and commitment, providing bearings through the inevitable contradictions and emotional ebb and flow of engaging with a severely disrupted world.

Cultivating conversations

Conversations that build connection are the building blocks of productive climate engagement. But all too often climate discussions are being avoided, contributing to an eerie sense of disconnection to the urgency of the problem. One reason that discussions are difficult is because it is so challenging to think in a sustained way about climate emergency. It is too big and too disturbing. The mind stalls before the immensity of the crisis and its existential threat.

In 2009 Jonathan Marshall edited a book called *Depth Psychology, Disorder and Climate Change*. What struck him most about the process was the difficulty contributors had in writing about climate change. He observed:

> Many of the contributors, including myself, repeatedly felt themselves being called to write, but blocked as to the actual writing in many different ways ... Promising starts flattened into halting ventures. Vagueness ... was common.... Our ideas often appeared disordered, disconnected, dislocated, disoriented, disjointed, disrupted, disorganised and sometimes disengaged. The chaos supposedly located within the external world leaked into a chaos of the internal world and was not easily separated out .... 'Internal' and 'external' mirrored and perhaps magnified each other.[25]

In addition, Marshall noted his own compulsion to write and write, often off topic, while other contributors wrote at length about how appalling climate change was, recapping what is known "as if the repetition will give us an order in which to act."[26] Ten years on thinking and talking about climate issues are still very difficult. Minds wander or go blank, deflecting jokes pop up, people preach or make bleak assertions, or someone says "this is all a bit too depressing, lets change the topic."

But another side to this story emerges when people are encouraged and supported to identify and share their emotional responses to climate issues in safe and contained conversation spaces. The reality is that many people really do want to talk about what is happening, especially when they feel they can safely share their fears, confusions and griefs. This is something I witness over and over again at conferences and seminars on climate change, where sadly spaces for such conversations are generally not made in the programme, but are snatched wherever possible. Safe and contained spaces for conversations are ones where people can speak thoughtfully and be listened to respectfully, where differences can be aired without argument, difficult questions asked, honesty valued, stories shared, silences respected and time taken to acknowledge feelings and to develop tentative meanings and strategies for sustained engagement. It is also where we find out we are not alone in what we are thinking and feeling in response to climate disruption. We are all in uncharted territory, looking for words to describe what we, as a species, have not experienced before.

In recent years I have been fortunate to be involved in numerous exploratory conversations in designated safe spaces, both in one-off discussions and ongoing ones, including an online depth psychology group which meets to share conversations and dreams about climate and other ecological disruptions. These groups, like the research group I facilitated in 2011, are containers for slow, thoughtful and moving conversations that nurture and sustain participants in their immersion in climate issues. They are heartening and moving dialogues, made safe by a group commitment to listen to others respectfully, without interruption, and to withhold criticism and judgement in response. An agreement of confidentiality also helps to maintain feelings of safety and intimacy. Within this safe environment, participants can delve into the dilemmas and unknowns of climate disruption with others. Sharing stories, dreams, poems and imaginings in particular brings feeling and creativity into discussions, enabling transformative shifts for participants and the group as a whole. What makes these conversations possible is an agreement that participants are there to identify and explore their responses to the climate crisis rather than to debate, organise or proselytise. While these forms of communications are all necessary for climate action, they can often mask feelings which hinder ongoing engagement, if not acknowledged.

Climate discussions, of all sorts, need to be done with great care and consciousness about how potentially traumatising they can be. Feelings of hopelessness, helplessness, paralysis or numbness are all traumatic responses which can swamp people when they hear about the climate crisis. When people are traumatised they cannot respond effectively to threats. They may also talk about what has been traumatising to them in ways that can then traumatise and alienate others. When this happens climate despair can become infectious, immobilising individuals and groups.

In order to help people not to become stuck in traumatic effects, climate discussions need to provide participants time and support to digest the bad news, acknowledge the upsetting feelings this stirs, reformulate different understandings about themselves and their lives, and identify solutions and actions. What is most important is cultivating relationships with others, both within the discussion space and beyond it. Through talking, listening and sitting together, people can encounter different ways of thinking and feeling in response to climate disruption. This connectedness allows distressing thoughts and feelings to be brought into consciousness. They can then be explored and become part of a transformative process that helps to be present with, and even curious about, what is happening in themselves and with others, rather than to defensively block against what is so disturbing.

Even in large demonstrations on climate disruption it is helpful to make space for a conscious acknowledgement and expression of the depth of people's feelings. In 2016, I attended a large climate rally in Sydney. There were many speeches, telling us how bad the situation was, ending with exhortations to act. As this progressed, I felt my mood and the mood of others around me lower. Fear, despair and grief stirred but there was no acknowledgement of this or space for its expression. But then it was announced there would be a minute's silence to mark the death and losses of climate change. Tens of thousands of people readily fell into a silence that was palpable. Although there were no words, there was connection through the collective acknowledgement of grief. At the end of the minute, a solo didjeridu sang out from the stage, earthy guttural drones with piercing wails, expressing for the whole crowd what was felt but had not been given expression until now. In this music I heard grief, endurance, power and a call from Earth.

It seemed I was not the only one to be deeply affected by this simple and moving ritual. These few minutes of shared mourning and ritual brought about a catharsis. The uneasy despairing mood of the crowd transformed. Spirits lifted and people bonded. The march that followed was joyful and energetic, peppered with music, rallying cries, jokes and spontaneous conversations with onlookers. Climate engagement needs times of shared catharsis like this, when inarticulate or overwhelming emotions can be expressed, through words, music, silence, image, movement or ritual. This acknowledges distressing feelings in ways that renew the appetite for an ongoing commitment to what really matters.

Individuals and their communities mature when they can be open and responsive to a complexity of feelings in themselves and others. We become stronger by exploring the contradictions and confrontations of our emotional lives in the safe company of others. For climate engagement to flourish, we need dialogues and exchanges that honour all of our ways of knowing, especially feeling and intuitive modes of understanding, which are often marginalised, if not denied, within public discussions and debates.

Without voicing our feelings and intuitions, people struggle to remain present, let alone fully functioning, in response to a challenge that requires all of our faculties to respond with commitment, creativity and care.

Bridging divides

So many debates provoked by climate change are oppositional and binary in their approaches, highlighting conflicts within ourselves, and between ourselves. In these struggles we can see old and new myths butting into one another. In the transitional zone between old and new myths, choices and decisions become more contested as previously fixed values and meanings are freed from their former moorings. Positions can be fiercely held in unstable times as people seek security in their firm views and certainties. Arguments are fuelled by intense feelings of threat, often unconscious, as thoughts and feelings about radical change and existential danger become too disturbing to entertain, arousing unbearable emotions of fear and grief. For climate denialists, dismissal of climate disruption is a protective mechanism that rational argument and scientific data cannot penetrate. Whether it is consciously acknowledged or not, they feel the threat to their worldviews and indeed their lives. When people perceive this level of attack, they can shoot the messenger in an attempt to safeguard feelings of security, no matter how ill-founded. Climate campaigners, of course, can also feel they are fighting for their lives, as well as for the generations to come. This can make for aggressive and defensive exchanges at times, if all sight of common ground is lost and people feel their backs against the wall.

Increasing collective action that can help mitigate and adapt to climate disruption is the ultimate goal. To help people engage in necessary social and technological changes, in ways that don't escalate into a shouting contest about competing worldviews and beliefs, requires skilled communication strategies – especially, good listening skills. These are ones which can step back from framing the problem in ways that unnecessarily antagonise significant portions of the population. More effective approaches de-escalate conflict, through emphasising a commonality of concerns, and a willingness to listen and empathise.

One leader in the area of climate communication is Katherine Hayhoe, an American atmospheric scientist and evangelical Christian. She suggests that rather than insisting on framing climate disruption as an ecological issue, it is more productive to show that it is an issue that relates to whatever it is that the person most cares about:

> So rather than feeling like we have to instil *new* values into people ... you need to enter the conversation as if the person you're speaking with has *exactly* the right values they need to care about climate change; that in fact, they're the perfect person to care and act.[27]

Hayhoe also advises against engaging with the arguments of deniers, because it's a lot easier for people to talk about having a problem with the science than the real problems of climate crisis. Instead, she advocates initiating discussions based on common values which may be humanitarian, health, security or economic. She talks to people about what they love about their area, or to Christian college students about their "belief that God created this amazing world and gave it to us to love and care for."[28] Focusing on these values increases people's capacity to welcome change as long as their worldviews are not directly challenged.

Hayhoe's approach works through connection, empathy and a commitment to positive outcomes, relinquishing any investment in being right. The biggest lesson she has learned, she says, "is that if we want hearts to change, we have to learn to communicate from our hearts rather than our heads."[29] She pragmatically presents climate issues to people as a human issue that's "already affecting everything else on your priority list: your kids, your recreation, what you eat, whatever industry you work in." It's an approach that grounds the situation in ways that sidestep debates, and prioritise action. In Hayhoe's experience, the most palatable solutions "make people feel like the better versions of themselves – more pragmatic, more competitive, more innovative, maybe even more fiscally conservative!"[30] They make a difference and are consistent with their identities. One solution she offers churchgoers, for example, is to cut down energy use or install solar panels so the church can fund more mission work. By shifting the framing of the issue, it goes from being a non-negotiable to something desirable.

Communicating about climate issues is more effective when linked to achievable actions that work towards solutions, helping to allay anxiety by channelling fears into constructive forms of response. This does not mean promising false hopes through magical remedies, but rather promoting solutions linked to collective actions that can make some difference to outcomes, whether they are short term or long term, local or global in scope. In the rural Northern Rivers Region of New South Wales, Australia, a successful campaign to stop fracking began with door-to-door conversations which showed that 94.9% of residents wanted their area to be gasfield free. Building on this consensus and supported by skilled community building efforts, a highly diverse community of farmers, Indigenous people, environmentalists, townsfolk, professionals and businesspeople united through a network of groups to embark on a path of non-violent direct action.[31] The campaign culminated in the Bentley blockade supported by thousands over four months, before all drilling licences were suspended and then bought back by the State government. A shared concern can transform people and their communities, especially when time is given to grassroots conversations and actions.

Empathy soothes tensions between different values systems, and old ways and new. This is why open and informal conversations between peers is crucial for engaging people and communities in climate action efforts. Stories from real life, compiled by Psychology for a Safe Climate in their excellent booklet *Facing the Heat*, give examples of how this can be done.[32] In it, they highlight a number of crucial factors in opening up discussions with those who may be initially resistant or reactive to talk of climate change. These include being patient, choosing the right time for positive connection, learning to de-escalate conflict, being curious about the emotions driving aggressive responses, listening to others with empathy and respect and seeking common ground. Given the complexity and intensity of feelings that talk of climate issues arouses, immediate outcomes can be unpredictable. However, open and friendly conversations can plant seeds of change in others which grow over time, as well as develop strategies and confidence to negotiate divides. A change of beliefs does not always have to lead the way to constructive conversations and actions.

Collaborative power

No one person can save the planet or ourselves from climate catastrophes, unlike in the movies. It is important to keep this in mind when committing to climate action. Both because the sense of urgency and pressure to act is high, and because the archetype of the warrior/hero is so dominant in contemporary cultures. The fantasy of global problems being solved in a flash by superheroes, whether they be

Spiderman, Wonder Woman or Richard Branson, is anything but a realistic model for action on the pervasive and complex causes and effects of climate disruption. Nevertheless, as Sophy Banks from the Transition Network observes, "the culture of the lone hero pervades even the most radical movements for positive change," contributing to unbalanced situations where leaders take on too much power and work.[33] When this happens, collaborative efforts become devalued and sidelined.

Letting go of heroic expectations that some powerful person will fix the problem, or that you have to be super powerful to act on climate issues, lays the foundations for building collaborative power from collective actions. Individuals can focus on what they can do with others, rather than project their expectations for action on to others, while social movements increase resilience through shared work and vision. As social creatures, humans find empowerment through interaction with others. Networked power is inspired and symbolised by ecosystems, like coral reefs or rainforests, where communities thrive through a web of interdependent actions.

Some twenty years ago, climate psychologist Per Espen Stoknes had a dream about what it meant to be an activist. In his dream, Stoknes met Picasso who showed him a painting of a Picasso-style tree bending in strong winds. Picasso told him "Its's titled *Activist*." Stoknes understood from looking at the painting that the real activist was not the tree, but "the wind who is the activator, bringing the tree into movement."[34] Linking the natural force of the wind to the work of being an activist provides Stoknes with a symbolic image and an embodied sense of how activism can be guided by natural forces. He writes "I can let myself be blown through by this larger flow – my responses, shaped, bent, and sustained by my way of standing in this vibrant current." This sustaining image inspires a collaborative sense of power that is buoyed and guided by the world's natural currents.

Environmentalist Tim Flannery also sees the potential for human collaborative action through a naturalist's lens. He suggests that humans are in the process of forming a global super-organism which is not yet mature.[35] This is both a biological and mythic view which highlights the potential for a human evolutionary process that develops identities and values based upon the overall wellbeing of our species and planet. Flannery's suggestion heads in the same direction as Joseph Campbell's anticipation of the emergence of a global myth that supports an individual maturing within the fabric of a global society through cultivating a conscious positive relationship to nature and cosmos. An ecosystemic worldview supports identifying common concerns, sharing resources and cultivating multiple perspectives. In global human terms, this means that every person on this planet has an interest and a role to play in social and ecological change. This inclusive view empowers individuals through connection, collaboration and daily actions. The climate movement 1 Million Women is a great example of this. It recognises the power that women around the world hold collectively because they make most of the choices about household spending and work. Its strategies aim to achieve both carbon reduction and the further empowerment of women through group support, education and action. Founder, Natalie Isaacs, observes empowerment does not stay contained but spills over into every aspect of a person's life. This is just as true for communities as for individuals.[36] One area of change feeds into many other changes, magnifying the agency and effects of individual actions, in a myriad of ways.

Seeing beyond linear processes and dualistic beliefs about individual power and powerlessness is a vital step in the development of collaborative models of social change. While governmental leadership on climate action is sadly lacking in many countries, a momentum for change within a widespread mix of communities is synergistically building initiatives of shared responsibility and power. As slow and frustrating as this process can feel at times, it anchors permanent consciousness change in the collective. The shift from an individualistic perspective to a systemic one draws on the synergy and distributed intelligence of many people's focus and action. This pricks the inflationary bubble of heroic fantasies, facilitating personal transformation and a psychological maturity embedded in an ecological worldview.

Systemic understandings and complexity theory support creative engagements and community building that can go far beyond trouble shooting or problem-solving approaches. They also foster humility. By their very nature, systems resist control because any intervention always has unpredictable unintended effects. Systemic awareness instead helps to develop skills of observation, collaboration, a willingness to be experimental and flexible and a greater valuing of the common good.

Many climate initiatives are based upon systemic frameworks that inspire innovative and collaborative ways of working. One project is

Living Data, an "independent program of interactions between scientists and artists who share ways of understanding and responding to climate change."[37] Founded and led by Lisa Roberts as a contribution "to the imaginative feat of knowing ourselves as part of nature," this initiative presents data, iconography and stories, through collaborative exhibitions, presentations, conversations and publications. Typically, Living Data creations engage the senses and the heart as well as inform the mind. This has been transformative for many involved. Scientists have started to more openly present their artistic responses, while artists are studying science.

Lisa Robert's work is inspired by connection; between herself and others, between artists and scientists, between human and other species and between Indigenous and biological ways of knowing. This has supported her in letting go of inflationary fantasies about single-handedly changing the world in ways she would like. A few years into the process she observed:

> it's been so enlightening and empowering ... to realise, "No, I can't change the world as much as I'd like to". I'm released of that burden. I'm not overwhelmed any more ... as soon as I just focused on what I can do with the resources I have and the people I can work with, I felt empowered ... and I also realised that we're not alone. There are heaps and heaps of people who are attacking this problem from many angles and that's even more empowering.[38]

It can be very liberating to accept the limits of individual agency in response to climate disruption. However, this does not come easily for some, as it involves letting go of protective defences which hold on to the illusion of having mastery over threatening situations. But when this deflationary realisation does happen, it shifts attention on to systemic and collaborative ways of working with others, and with our world. It also breeds empathy. For Roberts, there is strength, stimulation and comfort in knowing she is one small part of a global effort, made up of people with diverse backgrounds, outlooks, skills and motivations.

Joining with others to address the climate crisis is a potent catalyst for reshaping an isolated experience of self into a connected one. At an existential level, this can give human life meaning, at a biological level it is an evolutionary necessity for our species to survive its own ecosystemic destructions.

Evolving in community

The philosopher and educator Paulo Freire understood the potential and necessity of activist groups and communities to incubate consciousness change – in individuals and in societies. Freire advocated balancing cycles of action with reflective dialogues which helped people to challenge and analyse problematic cultural views and their effects on individuals and societies. He declared that profound love for the world and for people, along with critical thinking, "which perceives reality as process, as transformation, rather than as a static entity,"[39] are essential components for creating positive social change.

Any kind of group that forms in response to climate issues can become a crucible for consciousness change if they can name and analyse the personal and cultural beliefs and values that climate engagement brings to the surface. When an individual or a group recognises distress or dysfunction as a symptom of unsustainable beliefs or a denial of some valuable aspect of themselves, it creates an opening for reflective dialogues about how to support one and other in developing a wider consciousness.

Finding ways to sit with and analyse climate issues from multiple perspectives, along with our reactions to them, is a crucial part of weaving together splits in our world and ourselves, and transforming cultural mindsets. It takes openness, time and sustained attention to birth new attitudes and ways of being. One initiative that is taking this on is the Anthropocene Transition Project (ATP) in Sydney which brings people together "in order to explore the nature of the changes required by the Anthropocene Transition."[40] One of its initiatives, facilitated by ATP founder Ken McLeod, is a Dialogue Circle loosely based on the work of quantum physicist David Bohm. Dialogue circles, as Bohm conceived of them, were groups that met for open dialogues without any set agenda or purpose other than to provide reflective space for exploring people's feelings and thoughts without judgement or argument. Participants are encouraged to take their time, feel into body sensations and accept times of silence in the dialogue as opportunities to deepen self-reflection. In the ATP dialogue circle, each speaker holds a "talking stone" in a similar way to the Native American practice of holding a "talking stick," ensuring that only one person speaks at a time without interruption.

My own experience, as a regular participant of the ATP monthly dialogue circle, is that it allows me to sink deeply into my feelings and thoughts in response to ecological and social crises, and to share this with others. The slowness and spaciousness of the process cuts through the busy-ness of my daily life and thinking. Participants' contributions to the dialogue build up a depth and breadth of experiences and understandings that goes far beyond individual perspectives, in ways that are frequently moving and transformational. By the end of an afternoon of exploring thoughts, sitting with feelings, sharing silences, noting physical sensations and sharing stories, participants invariably express gratitude for the experience as well as a renewal of energy for engagement.

Dialogue circles are just one example of creating forums for open exchanges about the stresses and insights stirred by climate engagement. Other forms can evolve through giving good amounts of time for "check ins" at meetings, film or book club discussions, group dinners or other regular social occasions. Another possibility could be through learning and practising mindfulness meditation together. Workshops and retreats designed to support people in a deep engagement with the ecological losses of our time are also increasingly available through groups such as Joanna Macy's Work that Reconnects, the Dark Mountain Project, the Joyality program founded by ecopsychologist Eshana Bragg and environmental activist Rachel Taylor, and the Deep Adaptation Forum set up by social change educator Jem Bendell. On the climate front, both Psychology for a Safe Climate and the Climate Psychology Alliance do ground-breaking work running conferences and workshops to explore and support people in their encounters with climate anxiety, despair, grief and burnout.

What I repeatedly see is that people are willing, and often very keen, to explore the emotional, philosophical and spiritual dimensions of climate action when given a safe space to do so. When this happens, feelings of connection build quickly as people find mutual recognition in what challenges, inspires and moves them. They also get to think together about what any one person may not be aware of, or have sidelined or repressed. Thinking and feeling together, people can be with what they cannot face alone.

Sustained climate action needs collaborative projects that excite people and provide opportunity for transformative dialogues. Climate collaborations have the potential to be cauldrons for profound social and personal change, when they recognise that part of the work is to discuss, develop and enact ecological consciousness. No matter what the size or scope of the initiative, the actions and conversations they generate contribute in a significant way to reimagining ourselves and our communities in relationship to global ecosystems. The more we join together to respond to and reflect on the climate crisis, the more we can birth, share and enact new stories about living in conscious relationship with our world's communities and ecosystems.

Notes

1 Knitting Nannas Against Gas. The Nanna Wrap. Retrieved from www .youtube.com/watch?v=ECiMVm1fyOo
2 Earth Matters. (2015). 3CR Interview. Retrieved from www.knitting-nannas.com/media/Earth%20Matters%20KNAG%2015%2002%2015.mp3
3 Ibid.
4 Thomas Berry in letter to Gary Snyder quoted in Kingsnorth, P. (2017). *Confessions of a recovering environmentalist.* London, UK: Faber & Faber, pp. 100–101.
5 Banks, S. (2016, Jan 5). How can we keep from burning out? *Resilience.* Retrieved from www.resilience.org/stories/2016-01-05/how-can-we-keep-from-burning-out
6 Chödrön, P. (2002). *When things fall apart.* Boston, MA: Shambala, p. 156.
7 Marshall, G. (2014). *Don't even think about it: Why our brains are wired to ignore climate change.* New York, NY: Bloomsbury, pp. 3–4.
8 Richardson, J. (2018). When the end of civilisation is your day job. *Esquire.* Retrieved from www.esquire.com/news-politics/a36228/ballad-of -the-sad-climatologists-0815/
9 Davenport, L. (2017). *Emotional resiliency in the era of climate change: A clinician's guide.* London, UK: Jessica Kingsley, p. 35.
10 Caldwell, G. (2010). 16 tips for avoiding climate burnout. Retrieved from https://grist.org/article/2010-05-12-coming-out-of-the-closet-my-climate-trauma-and-yours/#tips
11 Gillian Caldwell on Climate Advocacy Trauma – Part 1. Retrieved from www.youtube.com/watch?v=5KdAz8ejMGs
    Gillian Caldwell on Climate Advocacy Trauma – Part 2. Retrieved from www.youtube.com/watch?v=bjTupmuT5Bg
12 Caldwell, G. (2010). 16 tips for avoiding climate burnout. Retrieved from https://grist.org/article/2010-05-12-coming-out-of-the-closet-my-climate-trauma-and-yours/#tips
13 Murugan, A. Retrieved from www.earth.eu.com/and personal communication.
14 Shaw, M. (2018). Mud and antler bone: An interview with Martin Shaw. *Emergence.* Retrieved from https://emergencemagazine.org/story/mud-and -antler-bone/
15 Hoggett, P. & Randall, R. (2016, Dec 12). Sustainable activism: Managing hope and despair in social movements. Retrieved from www .opendemocracy.net/en/transformation/sustainable-activism-managing-hope-and-despair-in-socia/

16 McKibben, B. (2013). *Oil and honey: The education of an unlikely activist.* Melbourne, Australia: Black Inc., p. 14.

17 Ibid, p. 24.

18 Northover, K. (2017, Feb 25). Lunch with Tim Winton: Reluctant literary rock star. *Sydney Morning Herald*, News Review, p. 27.

19 Havel, V. quoted in R. Solnit (2005). *Hope in the dark: the untold history of people power.* Melbourne, Australia: Text, pp. 13–14.

20 Weintrobe, S. (2015, Apr 18). Hope resides in mending the human heart. Retrieved from www.sallyweintrobe.com/hope-resides-in-mending-the-human-heart-and-mind/

21 Ibid.

22 Climate Psychology Alliance. (2019, March 7). Radical hope. *Climate Psychology Handbook.* Retrieved from www .climatepsychologyalliance.org/handbook/301-radical-hope

23 Solnit, R. (2005). *Hope in the dark: the untold history of people power.* Melbourne, Australia: Text, p. 163.

24 Moore, K. D. (2017). One good turn. *Orion.* 35th Anniversary issue, p. 21.

25 Marshall, J. (2011). Climate change, Copenhagen and psycho-social disorder. *Portal, 8* (3), p. 7.

26 Marshall, J. (Ed.). (2009). *Depth psychology, disorder and climate change.* Sydney, Australia: Jung Downunder Books, pp. 416–419.

27 O'Reilly, K. (2018, Mar). Katharine Hayhoe reveals surprising ways to talk about climate change. Retrieved from www.sierraclub.org/sierra/katharine-hayhoe-reveals-surprising-ways-talk-about-climate-change

28 Dreifus, C. (2018). An Evangelist for climate science: Five questions for Katharine Hayhoe. Retrieved from https://undark.org/article/an-evangelist-for-climate-science-five-questions-for-katharine-hayhoe/

29 Bateman, T. (2018). Wisdom from a climate champion: A conversation with Katharine Hayhoe. Retrieved from www.greenbiz.com/article/wisdom-climate-champion-conversation-katharine-hayhoe

30 O'Reilly, K. (2018, Mar). Katharine Hayhoe reveals surprising ways to talk about climate change. Retrieved from www.sierraclub.org/sierra/katharine-hayhoe-reveals-surprising-ways-talk-about-climate-change

31 Kia, A. & Ricketts, A. (2018). Enabling emergence: The Bentley blockade and the struggle for a gasfield free northern rivers. *SCULR 19*, 51–75.

32 Psychology for a Safe Climate. (2015). *Facing the heat: Stories of climate change conversations.* Retrieved from www .psychologyforasafeclimate.org/publications

33 Banks, S. (2016, Jan 5). How can we keep from burning out? *Resilience.* Retrieved from www.resilience.org/stories/2016-01-05/how-can-we-keep-from-burning-out

34 Stoknes, P. E. (2015). *What we think about when we try not to think about global warming.* White River Junction, VT: Chelsea Green, p. 225.

35 Flannery, T. (2010). *Here on Earth: An argument for hope.* Melbourne, Australia: Text Publishing, p. 274.

36 Isaacs, N. (2017, Mar 9). My personal journey on becoming an empowered woman. Retrieved from www.1millionwomen.com.au/blog/my-personal-journey-becoming-empowered-woman/
37 www.livingdata.net.au/content/about/about.php
38 Gillespie, S. (2014). Climate change and psyche: Mapping myths, dreams and conversations in the era of global warming. Retrieved from https://researchdirect.westernsydney.edu.au/islandora/object/uws:32281, p. 223.
39 Freire, P. (1972). *Pedagogy of the oppressed*. Middlesex: Penguin, pp. 77–81.
40 www.ageoftransition.org/our-project#!

Chapter 7

Re-storying Earth

Sharing dreams

Evolution happens most rapidly on the margins. They are wild and creative spaces, teeming with possibilities. Marginal zones, like shantytowns and marshes, are places where norms are weak and experimentation is strong. In the realms of consciousness, the margins are where exiled truths, dreams and imaginings lurk, unconfined by the limitations and blind spots of habitual thought, behaviour and social conditioning. Storyteller Martin Shaw observes that "if there's a crisis in the story, the remedy for the crisis always comes from the edge not the center."[1] To find our way in a climate disrupted world we must pay heed to the margins of consciousness, to the dreams, visions and imaginings that are vehicles for instinctual awareness, intuitive insights and emergent understandings that reveal possibilities for a wildly different kind of life.

Throughout human history imaginal life has helped people to liberate their thoughts and feelings from conventional restraints and to challenge the status quo. Dreams, visions and imaginings, with their symbolic language, have the potential to name the unthinkable, solve the insoluble, and give birth to new stories. Australian author Helen Garner writes:

> ... the unconscious works in us and for us, ceaselessly, with its saving complexity and its deep knowingness.
>
> Sometimes it seems to me that, in the end, the only thing people have going for them is imagination. At times of great darkness, everything around us becomes symbolic, poetic, archetypal. Perhaps this is what dreaming, and art, are for.[2]

In times of crisis, when breakthrough is the only way forward, paying attention to our dreams and imaginings is crucial evolutionary work. The dreaming psyche reaches beyond rational thinking processes, widening the margins of consciousness by tapping into instinctual knowing and inventive possibilities. "The dream is central to our evolutionary inheritance," writes Robert J. Lifton, "More than ever we must dream well if we are to confront forces threatening to annihilate us and if we are to further the wonderful, dangerous, and always visionary human adventure."[3]

One of the reasons that dreams are so valuable is that they disrupt the censorship of the conscious mind, re-storying ourselves and our world from a broader and deeper knowing. The symbolic images and narratives of dreams can express suppressed conflicts, fears and threats, as well as healing and guidance. The value of dreams and visions is well honoured in traditional cultures, but often marginalised in modernist cultures where scientific methods and monetary values have mostly excluded subjective experience as a valid form of knowing. Notwithstanding this, a number of scientific breakthroughs have emanated from dreams, including Alfred Russel Wallace's theory of evolution (before Darwin), Niels Bohr's discovery of the structure of atoms and Dimitri Mendeleev's formulation of the periodic table of elements.[4]

Dreams can and do change minds and the world. The inspiration for nonviolent protests in the streets of India came to Mahatma Gandhi through a dream,[5] while the Underground Railroad routes for runaway slaves were dreamt repeatedly by Harriet Tubman.[6] The dreaming mind activates the social and creative parts of the brain, thinking in ways that can elude the conscious mind. According to dream researcher Susannah Benson "Modern dream studies, do seem to show that dreams can have an adaptive, anticipatory function" which can "provide insight and illuminate issues or areas of concern as well as point to new pathways and areas of potential growth and creativity."[7] By paying attention to our dreams, that which dwells on the margins of consciousness can guide us towards what we need to know and where we need to go.

Not surprisingly, when I ask people about any dreams they have had that seem related to climate change, I hear many nightmares, particularly ones that feature floods, rising sea levels and massive waves. These dreams give urgency to scenarios of increasing risk in our heating-up world while also symbolising uncontainable and overwhelming feelings of anxiety through images of rising and flooding waters. In his research into nightmares, Kelley Bulkeley found that they "usually do more than simply mirror a person's conscious concerns. Most frightening dreams also include glimpses of possibility and alternative approaches to the threats and conflicts in waking life."[8] This was certainly true of the nightmare I recounted in the first chapter of this book. While my dream horrified me with its catastrophic vision of global sea level rises, it also revealed to me the necessity of immersing myself in this chaotic world, exchanging detachment for connection and compassion.

Dream sharing can deepen discussions in ways that might otherwise be avoided, consciously or unconsciously, sparking unexpected insights and emotional shifts. For these reasons, I was keen to include dream sharing in my research into psychological responses to climate engagement. However, I did not know whether the people who volunteered to be part of this research would respond to my invitation to share dreams they felt might be relevant to our discussions. Fortunately, participants did choose to share some dreams, helping the group to acknowledge and discuss what might have otherwise been "no go" zones, such as experiences of death, and feelings of despair, disconnection and trauma. We found these conversations strengthened and freed us to think together about what was too hard to face alone. The symbolic nature of dreams also helped us to be imaginative in our approach to emotional challenges, so we could identify both feelings and multiple possible responses drawn from the dream's imagery and narratives.

One dream image that inspired the group was shared by Lisa Roberts. In it she was tenderly nursing twin babies, one black and one white. This dream intrigued and moved the group. Its symbolic imagery of holding and loving both black and white, nourished ongoing conversations about the value of holding the tension between opposing views, emotional responses and social needs. These conversations helped to formulate and strengthen an intention to develop more conscious ways of exploring polarities provoked by climate change discussions with as little judgement as possible. It was an intention that held us in good stead whenever dualistic thinking and judgements surfaced in our conversations. Instead of falling into habitual patterns of thinking *either/or*, we learnt to consider *both/and* as a way to move beyond split and divisive thoughts. This enabled us to develop greater tolerance and compassion whenever our discussions did evoke conflicting feelings, views and judgements, both between ourselves and within ourselves.

An image or story that expresses more than can be consciously understood or verbally articulated, works symbolically. Symbols can be a catalyst for consciousness change as they aid us in recognising and feeling the larger dimensions of life, as well as what is currently unknown or unsayable. They have a transformative energy that motivates people on many levels of being, reaching beyond the limits of rational thought. Symbolisation, however, is a subjective experience. One person's symbol may merely be a descriptive sign for another person. For example, a national flag can evoke complex feelings of pride, belonging, determination, willingness to fight or to surrender in one person, while for another it is simply an objective identifier of a particular nationality. But whenever something does take on symbolic resonance for a group of people or a society, it can provide energy for cultural transformation and resilience, as well as spiritual experience. Collective symbols exist in many forms, including images, stories, events, places or even weather patterns. For my research group, the dream image of a woman nursing a black twin and a white twin worked symbolically, providing inspiration and energy to resist judging situations, views or people in black and white ways. Consciously paying attention to this image as a group opened up both beliefs and feelings that we could lovingly embrace what seemed contradictory in ourselves, as well as between ourselves and others.

Transforming symbols

Collective transformations require symbols that inspire and sustain a collective change of consciousness. Symbols are complex and full bodied. They connect us to what is unconscious and mysterious in ourselves and our world, opening up territory that is beyond rational thought and understandings. For example, water is commonly conceived of symbolically as the giver of life. In many cultures, water is symbolised in ways that are central to religious and spiritual experience. Hindus venerate their rivers as deities, making pilgrimages for prayers and purification, while Christians use water in baptism rituals to seek rebirth and salvation in a life beyond Earth. Water symbolism is universally potent, working at what Jung called an archetypal level, because life depends on it as a primal source.

However, cultural approaches to water translate into different effects. For First Nations peoples who honour water as the source of life, there are powerful spiritual and emotional motivations to protect water. The protests at Standing Rock had enormous impact not only because of the numbers of people who were there, but because of the way that Indigenous leaders educated all comers about protecting water for all of life as a sacred duty, making prayer and ceremony central to the campaign of resistance. The wisdom that "Water is Life" underpinned the campaign. Each morning, protestors came together for a ceremonial predawn walk to the river to make offerings, led by Indigenous elders and water protectors.[9] What happened at Standing Rock has become a model and inspiration for other environmental protests worldwide to speak out about and celebrate the sacredness of water.

By contrast, modernist cultures, with their exceptionalist beliefs, tend to symbolise water as a "thing," which can be measured and allocated, while also being mysteriously unpredictable in its appearances and disappearances through flood and drought. When there were massive fish kills in the dried up Menindee lakes in New South Wales in January 2019, the State's Premier Gladys Berejiklian suggested it was an unavoidable occurrence because "we cannot control the weather."[10] Other right-wing politicians explained away the kills as the result of droughts that had always been a part of Australian experience, dismissing concerns about overuse of water for irrigation and climate disruption as unhelpful politicisations of the issue. Their explanations reinforced the symbolisation of water as both a resource for human use and a separate entity not affected by human beliefs or actions. The overall effect of this dual-edged symbolisation can only be ecological disaster.

The climate crisis highlights water and its symbolic meanings. Standing on melting ice, being flooded and running dry are all symbolic expressions of powerlessness that resonate in climate discussions and that are amplified by the growing frequency of communities experiencing these very realities across the world. Both the metaphors and the realities reflect the consequences of not tending to human–water relations. To counter this we need to consciously nurture water narratives that have symbolic resonances attuned to Indigenous and ecological worldviews of reverence, interconnection and restoration which encourage action and compassion.

Perhaps the most transformational symbol to emerge in modern times is the image of our Earth from outer space. This iconic image works symbolically through its paradoxical evocations of distance and intimacy, familiarity and mystery, limitation and vastness, and awe and fragility in response to our planetary home. A further symbolic resonance to this image has been constellated through its linking with James Lovelock's Gaia hypothesis which depicts the Earth's biosphere as a single living organism, bearing the name of an Earth Goddess.[11] Working together, the image and narrative vitally contribute to an emergent global worldview that depicts Earth as a sacred entity.

Collectively we are in the process of birthing planetary consciousness, reimagining ourselves, our assumptions and our world in radical ways. Symbolic perceptions of planetary "oneness" and "aliveness" are finding expression in both creative and destructive ways through varying phenomena, including economic and cultural globalisation, the development of the internet and climate disruption. Symbolic and mythic resonances inform, and are informed by, all the ways humans experience and understand global oneness. While the intricacies of climate science can leave many baffled or unmoved, images and stories that reveal the complex, interconnected nature of our planet are vital in helping people to intuitively grasp the inter-relationships between who we are, how we think, what we do and the life of our world. Ecological crises call out for us to bring consciousness to the symbolic dimensions of our understandings and lives so that we can craft meaningful restorative narratives.

Guiding myths

Myths are ever-present in human consciousness. Their metaphoric worldviews interpret, shape and guide individual and collective lives. While contemporary cultural myths with their narratives about what makes a good life can quickly come and go, some myths are perennial, anchored in archetypal stories about change embedded in the processes of nature. These are the myths that knit together the great cycles of life, death and rebirth. We cannot take them literally but we can find sustenance in the wisdom of their narratives, especially in dark times when prevailing personal and cultural myths crumble beneath the weight of new circumstances.

When myths become unworkable or irrelevant, we enter a frightening and confusing terrain. The transitional space between old and new myths is rife with imaginings of conflict, loss and death. In relation to climate disruption, a mythic perspective offers insight and compassion for what is at play in our psyches as we grapple with both literal losses, and the clash and crash of worldviews. Myths about the underworld are particularly resonant. Not only do they grapple with the rock bottom realities of death, grief and renewal, they also provide us with metaphors that resonate with literal dilemmas about forging the right relationship with fossil fuel treasures in Earth's underworld.

Mythic journeys of descent into the underworld have many tellings with their accounts of abductions, deaths, resurrections and returns. They are initiatory stories about having to experience death in order to be reborn with wisdom and maturity. The oldest recorded underworld myth recounts the story of the Sumerian Queen Inanna and her twin sister Erishkegal. It begins not with an abduction but a choice. Inanna, the beloved Queen of Heaven, chooses to attend the funeral rites of the husband of Erishkegal, the much feared and shunned Queen of the Underworld. Inanna knows this is the right thing to do. What she does not know, until she begins her descent to the Underworld, is that she will be required to pass through seven gates, at each of which she will be required to relinquish her trappings of power, followed by every last remnant of her clothes. Inanna protests but ultimately chooses to submit to this stripping, so that she may honour the dead and perform the rites of mourning. When she meets her twin sister, she is naked and bowed low.

In today's developed world, many have lived the life of Inanna with royal privileges of water, power, transport and food available on demand, along with endless consumer choices. Yet, just as Inanna knew that her twin sister's underworld realm was being denied and disowned, many of us have come to acknowledge that our queenly lives are out of balance; high on costs to others and our Earth, low in reverence for death and limitations. There are descents to be made and death rites to attend on the way to any initiation that strips away old assumptions how our life should be and how the world works. The further we go, the harder it gets. Many are prepared to get to the first gate and put out the recycling. But protests mount when we have to strip off energy-intensive lifestyles, relinquish privileged mindsets and meet the limits of personal autonomy.

Rites of passage are always gruelling as they shred habitual behaviours and cherished identities, to make way for understandings. Nothing less is required for a genuine growth in maturity, wisdom and an expansion of consciousness. Even when we choose to make an initiatory descent, there is no avoiding feelings of powerlessness or the reality of death, as old protective beliefs and assumptions die. Inanna's reunion with her abandoned and grieving twin sister in the Underworld does not go well. Erishkegal is enraged with feelings of abandonment and grief. She judges Inanna and has her killed and hung upside down on a meat hook. These days, climate disruption is holding many of us to account and hanging us out to dry as we confront the grief of species being lost, coral reefs dying, human death tolls rising and the lives of our children and grandchildren being endangered.

Yet, at the same time life in the Above World goes on. It is business as usual for many. When Inanna does not return from her visit to the Underworld, her handmaiden goes to the father gods for help. They abandon Inanna, having no wish to engage with the Great Below of the underworld. Only Enki, the compassionate god of wisdom, will act. He creates messengers from the dirt beneath his fingernails to travel to the Great Below to plead for Inanna. To engage respectfully with the underworld or with climate disruption requires compassion and a humility rooted in Earth's nature. Getting our hands dirty, understanding where our food comes from and where our rubbish goes breeds respect for the cycles of life, death and rebirth and an intimate connection with Earth, along with empathy for others.

When the humble messengers reach Erishkegal in her Underworld realm they respond empathically to her moans. "Oh, oh my inside," Erishkegal wails. "Oh, oh your inside," the messengers mirror back. Their compassion and companionship softens Erishkegal's grief and rage. She offers these creatures any boon of their asking. They request Inanna's corpse and sprinkle it with the food and water of life. She is resurrected, healed and transformed, born anew from the womb of the Underworld, through the witnessing of grief and the agency of compassion. Now initiated, Inanna can never again be innocent of death or place herself above the limits of life or Earth's cycles. She commits to visiting the Great Below yearly, or sending close kin in her place. Never again will Inanna and Erishkegal live in estrangement from one and other.

In her reflection on the mythic underpinnings of contemporary culture, Jungian analyst Christine Downing distinguishes between the *heroic quest*, with its treasure-seeking journeys into the unknown to struggle and conquer, and *rites of passage* with their initiations into the universal rhythms of life.[12] The lone hero is motivated by possibility, reward and a desire to overcome nature, while the initiate, guided by mentors, finds wisdom in surrendering to the necessary constraints of the natural and social world. Heroic myths become dangerously unbalanced when split off from initiatory myths that are grounded in humility, compassion and community. This imbalance is reflected in expansionist cultures that promote heroic narratives about defeating enemies and stealing treasure while failing to provide adequate rites of passages for their young. What results are cultures of entitlement, short on mature understandings about life's responsibilities and workings. While uninitiated heroes are reckless and self-serving, initiated heroes revere life and work for the common good. Their humility and compassion contain and direct their heroic impulses within a respect for life's processes. The more each of us can embrace the mythic task of undergoing initiation through facing into the destructions caused by ignorance of and disrespect for our planet's life, the more chance we collectively have of developing the maturity and strength to remedy our actions with Earth-based wisdom.

Immersive stories

The story of our living Earth is both old and new in its interweaving of traditional Indigenous and emergent ecological understandings. In his book *Climate: A New Story,* Charles Eisenstein heeds both sources, portraying Earth as a fabric of aliveness which is "sentient, conscious, and intelligent."[13] This living Earth worldview illuminates how the climate crisis is a consequence not only of rising greenhouse gas emissions, but also of a lack of care and respect for Earth's living body and organs: the wetlands, savannahs, forests, reefs, rivers and seas. This understanding helps climate action priorities extend beyond political action to curb emissions towards a broad range of community actions focused on protecting and regenerating ecosystems through knowledge and love. Such actions are already being undertaken at a local level in many places. And, as Paul Hawken's Drawdown Project shows, they could be extended to great effect, helping to sequester carbon while developing ecological consciousness.

The aliveness of Earth is both a mythic narrative and an experiential reality. Eisenstein challenges sceptics "to stand barefoot on the earth and *feel* the truth of it."[14] For those who might need more convincing, a hugely popular London art installation "We Live in an Ocean of Air," uses immersive technologies to extend possibilities for feeling Earth's aliveness. Participants use virtual reality headsets to simulate the experience of being part of the ecosystem of a giant sequoia tree, the largest individual organism on Earth.[15] In addition, heart and breath sensors track the participant's real-time breathing, making oxygen and carbon dioxide visible with each exhalation, while scents, breezes and temperature changes intensify the immersive experience. Participants are invited to "explore new senses, to see and feel the invisible as well as the ineffable fabric of the natural world."[16] There is a paradox about technology taking viewers on an emotional journey through our natural world. But from all accounts, this installation is a moving experience. While data was being collected from the monitors to help scientists analyse the emotional effects of the experience, gallery staff reported many visitors leaving in tears. There are many ways that artists, story tellers, ecologists and teachers can enliven our relationship with Earth. Embodied narratives burrow under barriers of assumptions, beliefs and disconnections. They can blow minds and open hearts to what has been forgotten or silenced, softening the ground for consciousness change, while seeding inspirations for action.

Many artists and performers are taking to the streets to stir responses to the climate crisis. In one weekend of 2018, a group of Indigenous-led grandmothers blocked five street blocks in San Francisco to give artists from different community groups the space to create street murals depicting solutions to climate injustices. "To build the future that we want," said Cata Elisabeth-Romo, a lead coordinator for the mural project "you have to believe in a little magic and imagination."[17] Meanwhile, in New York, artists dressed as sea creatures joined a climate protest, combining stilt dancing, ritual and improvisation to awaken awareness about human connectedness with marine ecosystems.[18] This work was produced in solidarity with *Unmoored*, an installation by Mel Chin, which invited pedestrians to use their digital devices to view a future submerged Times Square, jammed with boats rusting away while a new marine ecosystem evolved in response to global warming. Chin said of his installation, "It is not about convincing you to believe in climate change or not believe in climate change. It is there to provoke a question: How will you rise?"[19] One recent response to this question has come from Extinction Rebellion, a protest movement that uses street theatre to great effect, including mass "die ins" in museums and public squares. The eerie, silent, slow moving, white masked, red robed figures at their protests have been particularly striking, evoking ghostly spirits coming to warn or haunt us about the bloodshed of ecological destructions.[20]

The growing movement of art and performance in public spaces gives life to ecological crises in ways that engage mind, feeling and body, raising awareness and empowering protests. Their creative vision proceeds from connection and invites further connection. The more we can evoke and speak of the web of life, and our embeddedness within this, the more committed and coherent our responses to ecological crises will become.

Evolving ethics

"Where do we root our ethics?" once we discard the human/nature separation, asks David Haskall.[21] Dismantling myths about human exceptionalism opens the way to a very different take on ethical dilemmas about how to live a good and virtuous life on Earth. If we, as humans, are not exceptional to the rest of life on Earth, what is the significance or value of human life? What does it matter in the universal scheme of things if we humans evolve and then become extinct? Or that we dramatically alter the Earth's biosphere in the process? After all, the planet will continue evolving other forms of life in response to changing conditions, as it always does. Philosopher Clive Hamilton brands this kind of thinking as "*paleofatalism*, an existential complacency that settles over those who spend too long immersed in geological timescales."[22] Psychologically, it can also be understood as an unconscious way of protecting ourselves from feeling the grief and terror of species extinction. Nevertheless, learning to place human existence within planetary changes and eras is a crucial part of developing ecological consciousness. Beyond being either panacea or denial, this awareness can give meaning and compassion through valuing our individual and species significance as a networked part of ongoing life on Earth.

Consciousness of life on Earth as a community breaks down perceived barriers between human and other forms of life, crafting a story and an ethics of connection. Haskall writes "When we are awakened participants within the processes of network, we can start to hear what is coherent, what is broken, what is beautiful, what is good."[23] For him, an ethics of belonging to life's network emerges from both awareness and embodied experience. It requires learning to "unself," even if just a little, by moving towards the perception and experience of other life forms, whether they be fish or the river they swim in. De-centring ourselves in this way, we can experience ourselves as a part of something larger rather than simply apart.

An ethics of ecological belonging affirms the value of all life on Earth, revealing the ways that we diminish and harm our livelihood and selves when we hurt other life forms. It also requires us to acknowledge that the human species is collectively causing mass destructions and extinctions in the course of daily modern life. Self-protective, socially conditioned beliefs attempt to shield us from the heartbreaks of this understanding and the unpredictability of life. Consumer cultures in particular run on beliefs that we can "have it all," and "for cheap." These beliefs diminish us and curb ethical sensibilities because they deny the high social, psychological and ecological costs of these cultures. Challenging this by observing the impact of our thoughts and behaviours on ourselves and others is the start to creating an Earth-based ethics which accepts a world of interconnections and griefs. To support these ethics, we need to cultivate forgiveness of ourselves and others for the destructions that have occurred, and are occurring, as a result of ignorance, disconnection and denial. Compassion for ourselves and others is the foundation of ecological ethics capable of negotiating with the fundamental principle that all life forms are connected and responsive to one and other.

One of the first Western philosophers to grapple with ecological ethics was Albert Schweitzer. While living in Africa during the First World War, Schweitzer realised that the European worldview, along with its ethical stances, were inadequate and in decay, because they were "rooted in belief rather than in thought which penetrated to the real nature of things."[24] Eventually Schweitzer's loss of faith and angst gave way to a breakthrough in consciousness. In his autobiography he writes how, when boating through a herd of hippopotamuses:

there flashed upon my mind, unforeseen and unsought, the phrase "Reverence for Life". The iron door had yielded ... Now I had found my way to the idea in which world- and life-affirmation and ethics are contained side by side![25]

On the basis of this intuitive insight, Schweitzer understood that:

A man is ethical only when life, as such, is sacred to him, that of plants and animals as that of his fellow-men, and when he devotes himself helpfully to all that life is in need of help.[26]

Schweitzer's ethical approach recognises both the sacredness of the world and the purposefulness of living with an empathic connection with all of life. It accepts that while we cannot avoid harming or even killing to survive, we can learn to live honestly and meaningfully, experiencing at a profound level the ethical concepts and dilemmas that this throws up.

Writing about Schweitzer's approach to ethics one hundred years later, anthropologist Jonathan Marshall explores how it normalises and anticipates the necessity of ongoing dilemmas, conflicts, uncertainties and unpredictable outcomes in human–world relations.[27] Marshall observes that Schweitzer's approach requires us to embody an ethical attitude rather than adopt a code that aims to give predictable practical guidance about what to do in every situation. It means learning as much as we can about any given situation, acting appropriately in that situation, paying constant empathic attention to an action's effects on all life forms as a related whole. As Marshall observes:

> Easy and routine ethical solutions are rare, and may involve suppression of some level of awareness or harm. Living ethically is not easy, and we need to be aware of the conflicts we face, to do the best we can as we learn.[28]

One truth that ecologically based ethics reveals is that you can never get it all right, nor be complacent in our virtue. There is too much interconnection and complexity in the world to ever be sure of perfect and just solutions. Philosopher Timothy Morton speaks of his own feeling response to this knowledge as being one "of compassion, which has some kind of joy and laughter in it rather than this, 'Oh vey, let's put a Band-Aid on everything,' kind of approach."[29] He too accepts that while we cannot make everything right and fair, we can bring a compassionate awareness to all of life.

Cultivating ecologically based ethical attitudes based in compassion encourages us to connect with all beings, human and other. It requires us to face into ecological harms and find ways to act together. Ethical codes that impose set responses and hierarchies of worthiness risk bypassing feeling responses and entrenching prejudices. The development of compassion for all beings within an understanding of the flux and interconnections of Earth's ecosystems commits to ongoing connection and response.

Meeting disaster with resilience

A climate disrupted world is a place of both absence and presence. Loss and grief awakens the heart and sharpens the mind to all that is, and was and may never be again on Earth. Existential questions intensify, transforming values, ethics, identity and consciousness in ways that can nurture life and love in the midst of catastrophe. Rebecca Solnit's research on communities who have been through natural disasters, including New Orleans in the aftermath of Hurricane Katrina, reveals just how altruistic, inventive and purposeful people can be when ordinary divides break down.[30] The prevailing response to disaster, Solnit hearteningly found, is one of increased compassion, community action, selflessness and meaningfulness. Sadly, this is often underreported in media outlets which thrive on sensationalist accounts of isolated incidences of violence which can also occur in disasters at times.

"Disasters are extraordinarily regenerative," Solnit writes.[31] Like revolutions, their disruptions spur possibilities, experimentation and innovation as the constraints and norms of everyday life drop away. What Solnit so hearteningly observes in the extraordinary circumstances of disaster is how much people want to belong to stronger communities and to be involved in meaningful work. It is vital that, as climate chaos intensifies, we consciously grasp the creative potentials for social and psychological renewal when conventional systems and practices fail. This is the time to build communities anew. Solnit concludes:

> The paradises built in hell are improvisational; we make them up as we go along, and in doing so they call on all our strength and creativity and leave us free to invent even as we find ourselves enmeshed in community. These paradises built in hell show us both what we want and what we can be.[32]

These observations are not meant to glorify disaster, which by definition involves catastrophic losses and intense trauma. But it is a reminder that humans, like all species, have innate capacities for collectively working together towards recovery and renewal when calamity hits. Branches shoot from fallen trees, seed pods open in bush fires, displaced birds find new feeding grounds and humans develop purposefulness and relationships in times of disaster, more often than not.

Stories of restoration and renewal have mythic resonance, containing vital guidance for maturing and evolving through adversity. The potential for personal and social transformation when things fall apart is a story we need to tell often and act upon in response to climate chaos. One such story is told by community campaigner Annie Kia about her town of Lismore in northern New South Wales. Her story "Linkmore" tells the allegorical story of how her town was both the hub of a long and ultimately successful campaign to stop the opening of gasfields, and then a few years later was devastated by record-breaking rains and floods.[33] Of the campaign, she writes:

> amongst the hard stuff and the good, a tissue grew between them, a warp of purpose, a weft of connection. It grew between them, invisible, threaded through the districts, woven everywhere, looped between their houses and their families.[34]

And then when the rains came:

> the flood of help began. 80 people put their hands up to help. Then hundreds joined them, and hundreds more. So many people! But Linkmore people knew how to organise. In groups of 5, equipped, assigned roles and tools, they went into the homes and shops and helped clean mud and muck so that the sodden heart of Linkmore could start to beat again, and hope could start to surface, and the town could shine once more in starlight.
>
> And even now, on full moon nights, up on the hill behind the hospital, if you looked with a sidewise kind of look, you could see the silvery threads, the warp and weft, the tissue of connectedness still there threaded through Linkmore, shimmering.
>
> Because the tissue we grow to prevent the gasfield will also heal us from catastrophe.[35]

The more networks and resources that communities can foster before disasters strike, the more chances they have of recovery, and of fostering revolutions and innovations in response to climate crisis.

While Solnit's research highlights the potentials for social transformation when disasters strike communities, mental health statistics reveal the high toll of climate catastrophes on individuals, especially when not well-supported. For example, 30 to 50% of people affected by Hurricane Katrina suffered from PTSD, severe depression, anxiety or hopelessness, and suicides went up substantially.[36] The American Psychological Association reports increasing levels of climate change mental health-related problems, both as a result of disasters and of ongoing stresses.[37] As climate disruption intensifies, there is an urgent need to grow psychological resilience through establishing strong social support networks, climate action groups and accessible community practices that help to regulate emotions, such as mindfulness practice, yoga and gardening, as is already happening in many schools. Communities that can acknowledge and support people through their trauma, grief and depression increase their ability to use adversity as a catalyst for evolving new directions and meanings.

The work of building resilience for enduring trauma and embracing transformations requires helping professionals of all sorts to shift from Western-based models of care with their individual focus towards community-based therapies. If the major task of psychology is to address psychological distress and human suffering, then its theories and practices need to engage with individual lives within the context of their communities and our world. There is much work to be done in supporting the development of community-based initiatives that engage with the eco-socio-political factors that lie beneath the prevalent numbness, anxieties, addictions and denials of our times. Ecopsychology and climate psychology movements are on the frontline of this work. So too is the International Transformational Resilience Coalition (ITRC), founded by Bob Doppelt. The ITRC brings together leaders in mental health, public health, education, climate, disaster management, and religion and spirituality to help individuals, organizations and communities develop the psychological, social and spiritual resilience to not only survive climate disruption, but "to find new positive sources of meaning and hope in life that increase personal, social, and ecological wellbeing."[38]

I am finishing this book in Tathra, a small and vibrant community on the south coast of New South Wales that has been at the forefront of a push for renewable energy for over ten years. A year ago Tathra was ravaged by intense firestorms in unseasonably hot and windy conditions, destroying sixty-nine homes and hundreds of hectares of much loved bush in six terrifying hours. When Malcolm Turnbull, the Prime Minister at the time, dismissed any connection between the bushfire and climate change, local Councillor Jo Dodds filmed a powerful rebuttal standing amongst the burnt trees adjoining her property. Her grief and trauma are palpable as she describes the trauma of her community and the land. A year later, Tathra is still working through the traumatic effects of the disaster. Nevertheless, community spirit is strong and its efforts to transition to renewable energy have been ramped up further. Last night the local school hall was packed out at a meeting where the local group Clean Energy for Eternity passed a unanimous vote committing Tathra to 100% renewable energy by 2030.

Disasters alter the course of life for individuals and communities, and, in the case of climate disruption, for our Earth. Jo Dodds is keenly aware just how much ongoing support is needed to deal with catastrophic events driven by climate change. She also understands that recovery does not mean going back to how life was before. The trauma will linger on for years, the community and land irrevocably changed. Her commitment is to translate the trauma of bushfire into transformative action. Since the fire, Dodds has stepped up to the challenge of speaking out on the climate emergency, including on Bill McKibben's national tour of Australia. She has also become the Co-ordinator of Bushfire Survivors for Climate Action, leading protests outside Parliament House.[39]

What is so powerful in Jo Dodd's campaigning is her ability to reveal her vulnerability, as she acknowledges the trauma, loss and grief of herself and her community, at the same time as demanding and initiating action. She tells me that her new life as a campaigner is both challenging and has hit a "sweet spot" as it brings her love of writing and storytelling into the public arena. Her stories express what it feels like to live with full awareness of climate disruption, and to become a creative force for change in response. This is the challenge for us all, to not attempt to shield ourselves from the tragedies of climate crisis, but to find empowerment and connection through facing into them.

Transforming through diversity

The climate news is worsening as I finish this book. Ice melt is accelerating, permafrost is thawing and insect, fish and bird populations are plummeting. The latest IPCC report states there is a window of twelve years in which to act – radically – to attempt to keep global temperature rise to 1.5 degrees. I don't want to believe what I am reading but I know it is true. It is hard to find all the words for what I feel: horror, grief, acceptance, numbness are all in the mix. I wonder what I will dream in response. Will the nightmares return? Or will the unconscious throw up something unexpected, as it so often does. What is it that I am not seeing, and need to see in the face of the looming disasters?

One morning I wake from a dream which is cheeringly revolutionary and hopeful. In it, I am in Parliament listening to an older male politician speak. He is dismissing grandmothers as unsuitable for politics. I rise up roaring, outraged that grandmothers, so wise in experience, are being ridiculed as unsuited for power. Other women join me, shouting protests. My husband, standing behind me, calmly tells this dinosaur politician about the existence of legislation from the past which empowered grandmothers as leaders. To my surprise his voice cuts through. The politician backs down. Then a female parliamentarian on the other side of the floor stands to speak. She is an Indigenous woman. Beside her stands a companion, an older woman dressed in a blue robe who is a spiritual leader or elder connected to the sea. She holds a calm silent presence while the female parliamentarian speaks about a dream she has had. She tells us that if we want to know about her dream work methods, we can look it up on her website. I smile at the way she brings traditional knowledge together with digital knowhow. Here is a woman of power who respects intuition, experience and nature, while fully engaging with today's crises.

My dream does give me hope. Women's voices and Indigenous culture are at the forefront of climate action, encouraging connection and community as modernist myths of separation, human exceptionalism and endless growth become untenable. They are stepping up while the dinosaur men are backing down. Within days of this dream, I am buoyed by news of the rising impacts of the protests by Extinction Rebellion and the student strikes notably led by teenage girls, as well as the growing political leadership of women like US Congresswoman Alexandria Ocasio Cortez and the New Zealand Prime Minister Jacinda Ardern. There is a wave of grassroots cultural change happening which is making its way into places of power.

Ruling global elites are largely comprised of Western-educated white men, most of whom are embedded with fossil fuel interests and exceptionalist worldviews. The power of these elites, shored up by privilege and economic pyramid schemes, will be undermined as the seas rise, the deserts creep and bush fires rage. While many of those who are richly endowed in material possessions and privilege vacillate between denial and panic, those who know their wealth lies in community and ecological connectedness are working towards healing ourselves, our cultures and our world.

The basis of healthy ecosystems is diversity. The more variety of experience, observations and functions that make up the ecosystem, the greater the resilience. Human cultures are the same. The more diverse the threads, the stronger and richer the fabric, and the greater the creativity. The cultural fabric of today's world, with all of its richness and interconnectivity has immense resources to meet the challenges of climate crisis. And the voices of the marginalised, those most vulnerable to climate disruption, are the voices that have the most to tell us. Not only about what is being lost, but also about what can be redeemed, and how. Prominent in their ranks are First Nations peoples, grandmothers, children, ecologists, farmers, meditators, artists, poets, researchers, campaigners and many others practised in observation, collaboration, appreciation and experimentation. These are the new leaders who are carrying the seeds for survival and renewal in a climate disrupted world. Through their work, an Indigenous worldview that understands human life within the networks of family, community, ecosystems, Earth and cosmos is finding new forms of expression.

Climate driven disasters are ripping up the beliefs, behaviours and values of modernist worldviews, driving radical changes in culture and consciousness for more and more people. There are no simple answers or remedies. As Adrian Tait writes in a recent Climate Psychology Alliance newsletter, "Paradox is everywhere; we need fear and hope, tolerance and impatience, realism and vision, tenacity and letting go."[40] Ecological realities insist we regenerate ways of living closer to the basics of survival that have been marginalised, if not denied, in the expansionist rushes of industrialisation and globalisation. These basics of survival include not only water, breathable air and food supplies, but also love, empathy, creativity, gratitude and community. Finding life-affirming purposefulness as individuals and societies is key. "The world is already split open, and it is in our destiny to heal it, each in our own way, each in our own time, with the gifts that are ours," affirms naturalist Terry Tempest Williams.[41] The call could not be more urgent. To respond means finding a part to play that fits our world, our communities and ourselves, creating a life of existential and personal meaning.

The end of the climate emergency story is unknown. Each of us is a teller and a participant. The more perspectives and sensibilities we can bring to it, the richer the tale and its possible directions. We cannot choose the times we live in, but we can choose the stories we tell and live by. My hope is that this book will be one of many sources of stories and conversations that weave together visions and actions for healing our Earth, ourselves and our communities. Within this collective fabric of restorative response may you thread your way into a wise and tender way of being with the destructions and creations of our era.

Notes

1 Shaw, M. (2018). Mud and antler bone: An interview with Martin Shaw. *Emergence*. Retrieved from https://emergencemagazine.org/story/mud-and -antler-bone/
2 Garner, H. (2016). *Everywhere I look*. Melbourne, Australia: Text, p. 152.
3 Lifton, R. J. (1987). *The future of immortality*. New York, NY: Basic Books, p. 194.
4 Tatera, K. (2016, Jan 13). 5 dreams that led to scientific breakthroughs and innovations. *The Science Explorer*. Retrieved from http://thescienceex plorer.com/humanity/5-dreams-led-scientific-breakthroughs-and-innovations
5 Adams, C. (n.d.). Creative problem solving in dreams with Deidre Barrett. *The Spirit of Ma'at 3* (10). Retrieved from https://spiritofmaat.com /archive/may3/barrett.htm
6 Sabini, M. (2009). Community dreams: It takes a village to understand a dream. *IASD Journal*. Retrieved from www.asdreams.org/art icle-community-dreams-it-takes-a-village-to-understand-a-dream/?
7 Benson, S. (2019). Navigating the great transition. In B. Bright & J. P. Marshall (Eds.), *Earth, climate dreams: Dialogues with depth psychologists in the age of the Anthropocene*. Honolulul, HI: Depth Insights, pp. 115–138.
8 Bulkeley, K. (2016, Nov 29). Climate change nightmares: A sign of things to come. Retrieved from http://kellybulkeley.org/climate-change-nightmares-a-sign-of-things-to-come/
9 Thanissara. (2016, Dec 4). A living prayer. Retrieved from https:// oneearthsangha.org/articles/a-living-prayer/
10 Davies, A., Martin, L. & AAP. (2019, Jan 28). Menindee fish kill: Another mass death on Darling river "worse than last time". *The Guardian*. Retrieved from www.theguardian.com/australia-news/2019/jan/28/menin dee-fish-kill-another-mass-death-on-darling-river-worse-than-last-time.
11 Lovelock, J. (1979). *Gaia: A new look at life on Earth*. Oxford, UK: Oxford University Press.
12 Downing, C. (1991). *Journey through menopause: A personal rite of passage*. New York, NY: Crossroads.
13 Eisenstein, C. (2018, Sept 10). Initiation into a living planet. Retrieved from https://charleseisenstein.net/essays/initiation-into-a-living-planet/
14 Ibid.
15 www.artrabbit.com/events/mashmallow-laser-feast-we-live-in-an-ocean-of-air

16 Segreto, G. (2019, Jan 16). Review: We live in an ocean of air by Marsh-mallow Laser Feast at Saatchi Gallery. *The London Magazine.* Retrieved from www.thelondonmagazine.org/review-we-live-in-an-ocean-of-air-by-marshmallow-laser-feast-at-saatchi-gallery/
17 Calma, J. (2018, Sept 10). Grandmothers stalled the police as climate protestors created the largest street mural ever. *Grist.* Retrieved from https://grist.org/article/grandmothers-stalled-the-police-as-climate-protestors-created-the-largest-street-mural-ever/
18 Intervention: Ocean Blues. (2018, Aug 29). Retrieved from www.nolongerempty.org/event/laura-anderson-barbata-brooklyn-jumbies-ocean-blues/
19 Cascone, S. (2018, Jul 12). Artist Mel Chin floods Times Square with virtual reality art to sound the alarm on climate change. Retrieved from https://news.artnet.com/exhibitions/mel-chin-confronts-climate-change-times-square-virtual-reality-artwork-1317413
20 Heardman, P. (2019, Apr 26). The meaning behind Extinction Rebellion's red-robed protestors. Retrieved from www.dazeddigital.com/politics/article/44238/1/meaning-behind-extinction-rebellions-red-robed-protesters-london-climate-change
21 Haskell, D. G. (2017). *The song of trees: Stories from nature's great connectors.* Melbourne, Australia: Black Inc., p. 146.
22 Hamilton, C. (2013). *Earthmasters: The dawn of the age of climate engineering.* London, UK: Yale University Press, p. 205.
23 Haskell, D. G. (2017). *The song of trees: Stories from nature's great connectors.* Melbourne, Australia: Black Inc., p. 149.
24 Schweitzer, A (1954). *My life and thought.* London, UK: George Allen & Unwin, p. 182.
25 Ibid, p. 185.
26 Ibid, p. 188.
27 Marshall, J. P. (2016). Ecological complexity and the ethics of disorder. In J. P. Marshall & L. H. Connor (Eds.), *Environmental change and the world's futures.* Abingdon, UK: Routledge, pp. 48–62.
28 Personal communication.
29 Morton, T. (2014). Timothy Morton & Hans Ulrich Obrist: A conversation held on the occasion of the Serpentine Galleries Extinction Marathon: Visions of the Future. *Dis Magazine.* Retrieved from http://dismagazine.com/disillusioned/discussion-disillusioned/68280/hans-ulrich-obrist-timothy-morton/
30 Solnit, R. (2010). *A paradise built in hell: The extraordinary communities that arise in disaster.* New York, NY: Penguin.
31 Ibid, p. 22.
32 Ibid, p. 312.
33 Kia, A. (2019). The story of Linkmore. http://anniekia.net/the-story-of-linkmore/
34 Ibid.
35 Ibid.
36 Doppelt, B. (2019, Jan 15). Climate solutions must prioritize the human dimensions of the crisis. Retrieved from https://mahb.stanford.edu/blog/climate-solutions-must-prioritize-human-dimensions-crisis/

37 Clayton, S., Manning, C. M., Krygsman, K. & Speiser, M. (2017). *Mental health and our changing climate: Impacts, implications, and guidance.* Washington, DC: American Psychological Association, and ecoAmerica. Retrieved from climate www.apa.org/news/press/releases/2017/03/mental-health-climate.pdf

38 www.theresourceinnovationgroup.org/intl-tr-coalition/

39 Bushfire Survivors for Climate Action Press Conference www.youtube.com/watch?v=4LYP-p8pt7I&t=594s

40 Tait, A. (2019, Mar). Climate Psychology Alliance Newsletter we are school striking because we have done our homework. *Climate Psychology Alliance Newsletter.* Retrieved from www.climatepsychologyalliance.org/news/newsletters

41 Williams, T. T. (2012). *When women were birds.* New York, NY: Picador, p. 228.

Recommended reading and resources

Climate psychology

A great place to start in on the burgeoning field of climate psychology is the website of the Climate Psychology Alliance www.climatepsychologyalliance.org where you find rich readings amongst its newsletters, blogs and papers. There is also an online Handbook for Climate Psychology www.climatepsychologyalliance.org/handbook/310-climate-psychology. Leslie Davenport's *Emotional resiliency in the era of climate change: A clinician's guide* (Jessica Kingsley, 2017) is a comprehensive and accessible introduction to the climate crisis and its effects on mental health, supported by case studies and therapeutic suggestions.

Jeffery Kiehl has a unique perspective to offer, being both a climate scientist and a Jungian analyst. His excellent book *Facing climate change: An integrated path to the future* (Columbia University Press, 2016) provides an overview of climate science and communication, along with an accessible introduction to facets of Jungian psychology. Two edited books on the climate crisis, full of diverse insights also rooted in Jungian perspectives, are Bonnie Bright's and Jonathan Marshall's *Earth, climate, dreams: Dialogues with depth psychologists in the Age of the Anthropocene* (Depth Insights, 2019) and Jonathan Marshall's *Depth psychology, disorder and climate change* (Jung Downunder, 2009) which can be downloaded from www.academia.edu/attachments/58751564/download_file.

For a focused in-depth analysis dive into Paul Hogget's edited collection *Climate psychology: On indifference to disaster* (Palgrave Macmillan, 2019) with its research-based studies grounded in depth psychology perspectives. Sally Weintrobe's edited collection, *Engaging with climate change: Psychoanalytic and interdisciplinary perspectives* (Routledge, 2013) is a stimulating read with wide-ranging discussions on individual and collective psychology and policy matters drawing upon psychoanalytic theory.

Climate communication and action

For an accessible short read on psychological insights and support for climate communication and action, download Psychology for a Safe Climate's booklets: *Let's speak about climate change, Facing the heat: Stories of climate change conversations* and *Coping with climate change distress*, all available on www.psychologyforasafeclimate.org /publications. Jane Morton's booklet *Don't Mention the Emergency?: Making the case for emergency climate action* gives an excellent summary of climate research on climate messaging, talking about solutions and emergency transition campaigns. Available as a free download from https://climateemergencydeclaration.org/climatemessaging/.

For a lively video introduction to the challenges and opportunities of opening up conversations about the climate crisis, go to Rosemary Randall's lecture "Climate, Psychology, Conversation" for the Cambridge Climate Lecture Series 2019 on www.youtube.com/watch? v=dqXtJt9OoLA. You can also find many excellent short pieces on climate communication on Renee Lertzman's website https://renee lertzman.com/essays/.

George Marshall's *Don't even think about it: Why our brains are wired to ignore climate change* (Bloomsbury, 2014) is an entertaining and thought-provoking exploration of climate denialism and climate communication issues. Per Espen Stoknes identifies psychological barriers to climate action and communication in *What we think about when we try not to think about global warming: Toward a new psychology of climate action* (Chelsea Green, 2015). His warm and thoughtful book is full of personal stories and strategic solutions for encouraging individual and social responses. Political adviser and climate campaigner Alex Evans gives a short insightful account of how stories and myths hinder or activate change in the *The myth gap: What happens when evidence is not enough* (Eden Project, 2017).

Rosemary Randall and Andy Brown's *In time for tomorrow: The carbon conversations handbook* (Surefoot Effect, 2015) is a helpful and accessible guide on climate action and communication, well-grounded in psychological insights and case studies. Another practical guide to communication and action, full of stories and case studies, is Nikki Harre's *Psychology for a better world: Working with people to save the planet* (Auckland University Press, 2017), based on social and environmental psychology research.

Paul Hoggett and Rosemary Randall's research paper on the psychological resilience of climate scientists and activists, "Engaging with climate change: Comparing the cultures of science and activism" is in the journal *Environmental Values* 27 (2018). Their insightful short paper "Sustainable activism: Managing hope and despair in social movements" (2017) can be found at www .climatepsychologyalliance.org/explorations/papers/201-sustainable -activism-managing-hope-and-despair-in-social-movements.

Ecopsychology, eco-despair and eco-grief

Vital signs: Psychological responses to ecological crisis by Mary Jayne Rust and Nick Totton (Karnac, 2012) is an edited anthology offering a rich read on a diverse range of topics and issues from ecopsychological and depth psychological perspectives. For a comprehensive understanding of ecopsychology as an emerging academic discipline and a professional practice, head to Andy Fisher's *Radical Ecopsychology*, 2nd edition (SUNY, 2013).

Joanna Macy's work has sustained generations of environmental activists. Her most recent books *Active hope: How to face the mess we're in without going crazy*, co-authored with Chris Johnstone (New World Library, 2012) and *Coming back to life: The updated guide to the work that reconnects* (New Society Publishers, 2014) co-authored with Molly Young Brown (New Society Publishers, 2014) are full of wisdom, stories and practical exercises for facing into environmental despair and grief and finding empowerment.

Rosemary's Randall's paper "Loss and climate change: The cost of parallel narratives" in *Ecopsychology* 1, 2009 is a seminal paper on psychological and social dimensions of climate change grief. Renee Lertzman's illuminating case study, *Environmental melancholia: Psychoanalytic dimensions of engagement* (Routledge, 2015) will appeal to academics and environmental communicators and policymakers.

The wild edge of sorrow: Rituals of renewal and the sacred work of grief by Fran Weller (North Atlantic Books, 2015) is a moving and lyrical guide to navigating grief in grief-denying cultures. Weller emphasises the importance of communal expressions of grief, particularly in relation to ecological destructions and losses, and gives practical guidance about how these might be set up and contained.

Climate change: analysis, solutions and the Anthropocene

There are many books now to choose from to get an overview of climate science and analysis, and the concept of the Anthropocene. These are just a few of my favourites. As a starting point, I recommend *Big world, small planet* by Johann Rockstrom and Matthias Klum (Max Strom, 2015) which explains the climate crisis within a framework of understanding about ecological planetary boundaries. Theirs is a holistic approach that combines scientific research with possible solutions, with a strong emphasis on the necessity of a global shift in worldview. Paul Hawken's edited book *Drawdown: The most comprehensive plan ever proposed to reverse global warming* (Penguin, 2017) takes a holistic approach to climate solutions in its proposals for drawing carbon out of the atmosphere as well as reducing emissions. It is a huge resource of information for how climate and specific ecologies work, and how humans can collaborate with ecosystems for planetary healing.

For a comprehensive socio-political analysis of the way economic systems, namely capitalism and neoliberalism, are driving climate disruption you cannot go past Naomi Klein's *This changes everything* (Simon & Schuster, 2014). Beautifully written and very thoroughly researched, it identifies both problems and solutions worldwide through analysis, case studies and stories about the way social movements are tackling the climate crisis by challenging destructive elites.

Lastly, Gaia Vince's *Adventures in the Anthropocene: A journey to the heart of the planet we made* (Milkweed, 2014) is a fascinating and moving account of her travels around the globe to visit communities who are suffering from some of the worst effects of climate disruption. Vince, a science journalist meets people and groups who are developing extraordinary solutions and resilience on the ground, while clearly explaining the geophysics and ecological science behind contemporary ecological destructions and threats.

Index